WITHDRAWN

PATRICK O'NEILL is a member of the Department of German
at the University of British Columbia, Vancouver, and the
author of <u>Alfred Döblin's "Babylonische Wandrung."</u>

Günter Grass is possibly the most important living German
author. The literature on Grass and his works has been
growing rapidly over the last two decades, in literary
feuilletons and scholarly journals, in social columns and
political broadsides. His writings are controversial: he
has received the highest plaudits from the literary critics on the one hand, while on the other, he has had to
defend himself against charges of pornography. For several years now a reliable systematic bibliography has been
an acknowledged need not only of the Grass specialist and
the student of modern German literature, but also of anyone seriously involved with contemporary world literature.

This is the most comprehensive, up-to-date, and best
organized bibliography yet published on Grass. It includes all of Grass's works, and all scholarly writings of
major importance published to the end of 1975.

The entries have been arranged so as to make the information easily accessible to the reader: works are
divided into primary and secondary material, then accord-
ing to genre, individual works, and chronologically. Also
included are separate sections on general biographical
sources, works in translation, and interviews with Grass.
A combined author and subject name index facilitates reference to both primary and secondary material.

<u>Günter Grass: A Bibliography 1955-1975</u> will be an in-
dispensable tool for scholars, students, and all others
interested in contemporary German and comparative literature.

Günter Grass
A Bibliography
1955-1975

PATRICK O'NEILL

University of Toronto Press / Toronto and Buffalo

© University of Toronto Press 1976
Toronto and Buffalo
Printed in Canada

PT
2613
, R338
Z5
1976

Library of Congress Cataloging in Publication Data

O'Neill, Patrick   1945-
Günter Grass: a bibliography, 1955-1975.

Includes index.
1. Grass, Günter, 1927- --Bibliography.
Z8366.48.053 (PT2613.R338) 016.838'9'1409
ISBN 0-8020-5362-9   76-17278

This book has been published with the help of a grant from
the Humanities Research Council of Canada, using funds
provided by the Canada Council, and with the help of the
Publications Fund of University of Toronto Press.

P R E F A C E

For nearly two decades Günter Grass has been a fact of German life, as novelist, dramatist, poet, artist, and vocal participant in the social and political affairs of the day. His list of publications since 1955 now exceeds four hundred items. The volume of critical literature devoted to Grass has also been rapidly growing, in monographs and in scholarly journals as well as in social columns and political broadsides. For some time now a reliable, comprehensive, and systematic bibliography has been an acknowledged need not only of the specialist in modern German literature, but of anyone seriously involved with contemporary world literature. Grass can be—and frequently has been—attacked, but he can hardly be avoided.

There have been several previous bibliographies devoted to Grass, though only one, Everett (entry number 510), is of book length. Of the others—none of them longer than twenty pages—Wieser (500), Loschütz (501), and Schwarz (502) are useful mainly for popular German reaction to the earlier works, Görtz (505) and Kaufmann/Görtz (506) for reaction to Grass's political activities, while Woods (507, 508) is the first to pay due attention to North American criticism, frequently radically different from that of German critics. Everett, in effect, extends the coverage to the end of 1971. All of these bibliographies are selective, though to different degrees and in different fashions.

The present work also lays no claim to completeness as far as secondary literature is concerned. Grass as celebrity and politician is the object of a continuing barrage of ephemera and trivia, the collection of which here would serve little purpose. Even from a more strictly literary point of view—the primary focus here—Grass's works have been translated into everything from Catalan to Slovenian, Finnish to Japanese. Local reaction to these translations—other than English and, to a much lesser degree, French—is almost entirely unrepresented. What is laid claim to here is comprehensiveness: to the extent that all critical and scholarly works of major importance have been included. For the rest the emphasis is naturally on German-language and English-language (especially North American) criticism.

Where possible items have been physically verified.

The arrangement is chronological within the individual sections both in the primary and secondary divisions—within the individual years the arrangement is alphabetical. Coverage extends to the end of 1975. The index is a combined author and subject name-index and refers to both the primary and secondary divisions. For convenience of reference entries numbered lower than 500 refer to primary material, those numbered from 500 refer to secondary material.

My thanks are due mainly to the Library of the University of British Columbia, especially its Interlibrary Loan department; the Deutsches Literaturarchiv, Marbach am Neckar; the Research Committee of the University of British Columbia for financial assistance towards the preparation of the manuscript; the Humanities Research Council of Canada for financial assistance towards its publication; and my wife for bearing with nearly four years of card-shuffling while I assembled it.

Patrick O'Neill
University of British Columbia
February 1976

C O N T E N T S

I. F I C T I O N

1 / Independent Publications

1 Die Blechtrommel. Neuwied: Luchterhand, 1959, 13th. edn.
   1969; Frankfurt: Fischer Bücherei, 1962; Darmstadt:
   Moderner Buch-Club, 1964; Zürich: Buchclub Ex Libris,
   1965; Stuttgart: Europäischer Buch- und Phonoclub, 1966;
   Stuttgart: Deutscher Bücherbund, 1966; Frankfurt: Bücher-
   gilde Gutenberg, 1966; Gütersloh: Bertelsmann Lesering,
   1966; Vienna: Buchgemeinschaft Donauland, 1968; Neuwied:
   Luchterhand, 1968 (bibliophile edn., illustr. Heinrich
   Richter); Neuwied: Luchterhand, 1974 (Sammlung Luchterhand 147: "Danziger Trilogie 1"), 3rd. edn. 1975.
2 Katz und Maus. Neuwied: Luchterhand, 1961; 8th. edn.
   1967; Hamburg: Rowohlt, 1963; Darmstadt: Moderner Buch-
   Club, 1964; Zürich: Buchclub Ex Libris, 1966; Waltham,
   Mass: Blaisdell, 1969, ed. Edgar Lohner; London: Heine-
   mann, 1971, ed. H.F. Brookes and C.E. Fraenkel; Neuwied:
   Luchterhand, 1974 (Sammlung Luchterhand 148: "Danziger
   Trilogie 2"), 4th. edn. 1975.
3 Hundejahre. Neuwied: Luchterhand, 1963; Darmstadt:
   Moderner Buch-Club 1965; Zürich: Buchclub Ex Libris, 1966;
   Gütersloh: Bertelsmann Lesering, 1967; Stuttgart: Euro-
   päischer Buch- und Phonoclub, 1967; Stuttgart: Deutscher
   Bücherbund, n.d.; Vienna: Buchgemeinschaft Donauland,
   1967; Hamburg: Rowohlt, 1968; Neuwied: Luchterhand, 1974
   (Sammlung Luchterhand 149: "Danziger Trilogie 3").
4 Örtlich betäubt. Neuwied: Luchterhand, 1969, 2nd. edn.
   1969; Stuttgart: Deutscher Bücherbund, 1971; Frankfurt:
   Fischer Taschenbuchverlag, 1972, 6th. edn. 1975.
5 Aus dem Tagebuch einer Schnecke. Neuwied: Luchterhand,
   1972; Stuttgart: Deutscher Bücherbund, 1973; Hamburg:
   Rowohlt, 1974.

2 / Contributions to periodicals and collections

1955

6 "Meine grüne Wiese." Akzente, 2(1955), 528-34; rpt.
   Deutsche Prosa, ed. Horst Bingel (Stuttgart: Deutsche
   Verlags-Anstalt, 1963), pp. 368-75; rpt. Deutsche zeit-
   genössische Literatur: Epik und Dramatik nach 1945, ed.
   F.M. Boesschoten ('s Gravenhage-Rotterdam: Nijgh and Van

1

Ditmar, 1968), pp. 89-95.

1958

7   "Die Linkshänder." Neue deutsche Hefte, 5(1958), 38-42;
    rpt. Deutschland erzählt, ed. Benno von Wiese (Frankfurt:
    Fischer Bücherei, 1962), pp. 280-84.
8   "Fernwirkender Gesang vom Stockturm aus gesungen." Mer-
    kur, 12(1958), 937-44.

1959

9   "Der weite Rock." Akzente, 6(1959), 2-12.
10 "Rasputin und das ABC." Akzente, 6(1959), 13-25.

1960

11 "Im Tunnel." National-Zeitung (Basel), 9 January 1960.
12 "Stier oder Liebe." Deutsche Zeitung (Köln), 9/10 Octo-
    ber 1960; rpt. under title "Eingemauert," Westdeutsches
    Tageblatt, 24 February 1962, and Stuttgarter Zeitung,
    27 May 1971, p. 50.

1961

13 "Das Taschenmesser, oder Die Weichsel fliesst." Akzente,
    8(1961), 196-206.

1962

14 "Harras macht Geschichte." Das Atelier, ed. Klaus Wagen-
    bach (Frankfurt, Hamburg: Fischer Bücherei, 1962), pp.
    41ff.

1963

15 "Zwei Fragmente aus dem Roman Hundejahre" (Schneemänner,
    Der Knochenberg). Neue Rundschau, 74(1963), 165-93.

1972

16 "Die Kinder der Melancholia. Aus dem Tagebuch einer
    Schnecke." Die Zeit, 9 June 1972, p. 14.
17 "Ich bin ein Revisionist. Aus dem Tagebuch einer
    Schnecke." Deutsches Allgemeines Sonntagsblatt, 9 July
    1972, p. 24.
18 "Und was issen Fortschritt? Aus dem Tagebuch einer
    Schnecke." Stuttgarter Zeitung, 5 August 1972, p. 50.
19 "Enthäuptung einer Person. Aus dem Tagebuch einer
    Schnecke." Frankfurter Allgemeine Zeitung, 8 August

1972, p. 18.
20 "Aus dem Tagebuch einer Schnecke." National-Zeitung
    (Basel), 12 August 1972, p. III.

II. D R A M A

1 / Independent Publications

21 Hochwasser. Frankfurt: Suhrkamp, 1963 (edition suhrkamp).
22 Onkel, Onkel. First performance 1958, Bühnen der Stadt
    Köln; revised version: Berlin: Wagenbach, 1965.
23 Die Plebejer proben den Aufstand. Neuwied: Luchterhand,
    1966; Frankfurt: Fischer, 1968 (Fischer Bücherei), 8th.
    edn. 1975; London: Heinemann, 1971, ed. H.F. Brookes and
    C.E. Fraenkel.
24 Hochwasser and Noch zehn Minuten bis Buffalo. Ed. A.
    Leslie Willson. New York: Appleton-Century-Crofts, 1967.
25 Theaterspiele. Neuwied: Luchterhand, 1970; Hamburg:
    Rowohlt (rororo), 1975 (Contains: Hochwasser, Onkel,
    Onkel, "Noch zehn Minuten bis Buffalo," "Die bösen Köche,"
    Die Plebejer proben den Aufstand, Davor).
26 Davor: Ein Stück in 13 Szenen. Student edn. ed. Victor
    Lange and Frances Lange. New York: Harcourt Brace
    Jovanovich, 1973.

2 / Contributions to periodicals and collections

1957

27 "Die Grippe. Ein Spiel in einem Akt." Neue Deutsche
    Hefte, 4(1957/58), 35-44; rpt. Text + Kritik (Göttingen),
    No. 1(1964), pp. 16-24 (later incorporated as the first
    act in Onkel, Onkel).

1958

28 "Noch zehn Minuten bis Buffalo." Akzente, 5(1958), 5-17;
    rpt. Spiele in einem Akt, ed. Walter Höllerer, Marianne
    Heyland, and Norbert Miller (Frankfurt: 1961), pp. 533ff;
    rpt. Deutsches Theater der Gegenwart, ed. Karlheinz
    Braun, Bd. 1 (Frankfurt: Suhrkamp, 1967), pp. 351-68; rpt.
    Theaterspiele (1970).
29 "Beritten hin und zurück: Ein Vorspiel auf dem Theater."
    Akzente, 5(1958), 399-409.

3

1960

30 "Hochwasser." Akzente, 7(1960), 498-539; revised version
Frankfurt: Suhrkamp, 1963 (edition suhrkamp).

1961

31 "Die bösen Köche." Modernes deutsches Theater, ed. Paul
Pörtner, Bd. 1 (Neuwied, Berlin: Luchterhand, 1961); rpt.
Theaterspiele (1970).

1965

32 "Onkel, Onkel." (2nd. act, revised version) Konkret, No.
2(1965), 28-31.
33 "POUM oder die Vergangenheit fliegt mit: Ein Spiel in
einem Akt." Der Monat, 17, No. 207 (1965), 33-38; also
in Plädoyer für eine neue Regierung oder keine Alternative, ed. Hans Werner Richter (Hamburg: Rowohlt, 1965),
pp. 96-104.

1969

34 "Davor." Theater heute, 10, No. 4 (1969), 41-54; rpt.
Theaterspiele (1970).

3 / Unpublished dramatic works

35 "Zweiunddreissig Zähne." First performance 1959, Süddeutscher Rundfunk.
36 "Eine öffentliche Diskussion." First performance 1963,
Hessischer Rundfunk. Incorporated in Hundejahre (Neuwied: Luchterhand, 1963), pp. 571-613.
37 "The World of Günter Grass." Arranged and directed by
Dennis Rosa. Dramatization of excepts from Grass's
works, first performed under this title April 1966,
Pocket Theater, New York. Originally entitled "An album
of Günter Grass," and first performed under this title
February 1966, Pennsylvania State University.

4 / Ballets

38 "Stoffreste." First performed 1957, Stadttheater Essen.
39 "Fünf Köche." First performed 1959, Aix-les-Bains and
Bonn.
40 "Goldmäulchen." First performed 1964, Werkraum Theater
München.
41 "Die Vogelscheuchen." First performed 1970, Deutsche

Oper, Berlin.

III. P O E T R Y

1 / Independent Publications

42 Die Vorzüge der Windhühner. Neuwied, Berlin: Luchter-
    hand, 1956; 2nd. rev. edn. 1963, 3rd. edn. 1967.
43 Gleisdreieck. Neuwied: Luchterhand, 1960, 2nd. edn. 1967.
44 Selected Poems. New York: Harcourt, Brace and World;
    London: Secker and Warburg, 1966 (selected poems from Die
    Vorzüge der Windhühner and Gleisdreieck, together with
    English translations by Michael Hamburger and Christopher
    Middleton).
45 Ausgefragt. Neuwied: Luchterhand, 1967, 2nd. edn. 1967.
46 Günter Grass. Ed. and introd. Theodor Wieser. Porträt
    und Poesie. Neuwied: Luchterhand, 1968.
47 New Poems. New York: Harcourt, Brace and World, 1968
    (selected poems from Ausgefragt, with English translations
    by Michael Hamburger).
48 Gedichte. Ed. Heinz Schöffler. Darmstadt: Moderner
    Buch-Club, 1969 (selected poems from Die Vorzüge der Wind-
    hühner, Gleisdreieck, and Ausgefragt).
49 Gesammelte Gedichte. Mit einem Vorwort von Heinrich Vorm-
    weg. Neuwied: Luchterhand, 1971, 2nd. edn. 1974.
50 Mariazuehren. Hommageàmarie. Inmarypraise. Photographs
    by Maria Rama. Trans. into French by Emmanuela de Nora.
    Trans. into English by Christopher Middleton. München:
    Bruckmann, 1973. 88 pp. 75 illustrations.
51 Liebe geprüft. Bremen: Carl Schünemann, 1974 (biblio-
    phile edition of 150 copies).

2 / Contributions to periodicals and collections

1955

52 "Lilien aus Schlaf." Akzente, 2(1955), 259-60.
53 "Kürzestgeschichten aus Berlin." Akzente, 2(1955), 517.
54 "Polnische Fahne." Akzente, 2(1955), 535.

1956

55 "Aus dem Alltag der Puppe Nana." Akzente, 3(1956), 432-
    35.
56 "Saturn. Stapellauf. Zugefroren." Junge Lyrik, ed.
    Hans Bender (München: Hanser, 1956), pp. 27-29.

5

1957

57 "Klappstühle." Hortulus (St. Gallen), 7(1957), 178.

1958

58 "Gedichte: Im Ei. Frost und Gebiss." Akzente, 5(1958), 59-61.
59 "Annabel Lee. Kinderlied." Akzente, 5(1958), 387-88; 8(1961), 7-8.

1959

60 "Gedichte." Akzente, 6(1959), 483-87.
61 "Die grosse Trümmerfrau spricht." Der Monat, 12, No. 140 (1959/60), 19-21.
62 "Gedichte." Hefte für Literatur und Kritik (Wien), 1, No. 3 (1959-61), 18-20.

1960

63 "Zauberei mit den Bräuten Christi." Akzente, 7(1960), 48-49.
64 "Gedichte: Der amtliche Tod. Goethe." Akzente, 7(1960), 262-65.
65 "Die Erstgeburt." Akzente, 7(1960), 435.
66 "Gedichte" (Zugluft, Narziss, Mein Radiergummi). Merkur, 14, No. 149 (1960), 625-27.
67 "Brandmauern. Diana oder die Gegenstände." Du (Zürich), 20, No. 6 (1960), 16, 20.

1961

68 "Heringe." Akzente, 8(1961), 55-56.
69 "Fotogen." Akzente, 8(1961), 450.
70 "Siebenundzwanzig Männer." Alternative (Berlin), 4 (1961), 10-11.

1963

71 "In Memoriam Walter Henn. Mein Freund Walter Henn ist tot." Der grüne Wagen (München, Erlangen), 1963/64.

1964

72 "Kinderpredigt." In: Hannes Schwenger, Berlin zum Beispiel (Berlin: Staneck, 1964), p. 10.
73 "Vergleichsweise. Orpheus. Hymne. Allein." Die Meisengeige: Zeitgenössische Nonsensverse, ed. Günter Bruno Fuchs (Munich: Hanser, 1964), pp. 32, 85, 140, 174.

1965

74 "Duell mit dem Geier." Das schwarze Brett, 1 (Berlin: Wagenbach, 1965), p. 13.
75 "Der Mann mit der Fahne spricht einen atemlosen Bericht." Akzente, 12(1965), 122-23.
76 "Adornos Zunge." Akzente, 12(1965), 289.
77 "Kleckerburg." Atlas (Berlin: Wagenbach, 1965), pp. 26-30.

1966

78 "Der Neubau." Eckart-Jahrbuch, 1966/67, p. 16.
79 "März." Luchterhands Loseblattlyrik, No. 1 (1966), p. 4.
80 "Silberblick." Du/Atlantis (Zürich), 26(1966), 900.
81 "Vom Rest unterm Nagel." Kursbuch 7 (1966), pp. 9-12.
82 "Gedichte." Akzente, 13(1966), 200-207.
83 "Neue Mystik." Akzente, 13(1966), 578-79.
84 "Mein grosses Ja bildet Sätze mit kleinem Nein." Akzente, 13(1966), 481-89.

1967

85 "Vermont. Zwischen Greise gestellt." Mundus Artium, 1, No. 1 (1967/68), 24-27.
86 "Zorn, Ärger, Wut." Ein Gedicht und sein Autor: Lyrik und Essay, ed. Walter Höllerer (Berlin: Literarisches Colloquium, 1967), pp. 264-77.
87 "Vier Gedichte" (Ausgefragt, Grau, Sechsundsechzig, Liebe). Der Monat, 19, No. 220 (1967), 49-52.
88 "Ausgefragt." Forum, 14(1967), 383-87.

1968

89 "Tränentüchlein." Der Telegraf (Berlin), 14 January 1968.
90 "Die Schweinekopfsülze." Tintenfisch, 1(1968), 69-72; Hamburg: Merlin-Verlag, 1969 (poster).
91 "Danach." Luchterhands Loseblattlyrik, No. 14(1968), p. 3.

1971--

92 "Schreiben." In: Richard Salis, Motive (Tübingen, Basel: Erdmann, 1971), pp. 93-94.
93 "Hymne." Jemand der schreibt: 57 Aussagen, ed. Rudolf de le Roi (München: Carl Hanser, 1972), p. 77.
94 "Todesarten: Als Ingeborg Bachmann starb." Die Zeit, 26 October 1973, p. 18.

3 / Translations by Günter Grass

95   O Susanna: Ein Jazzbilderbuch. Berlin: Kiepenheuer und
     Witsch, 1959.

IV. T H E O R E T I C A L ,   P O L I T I C A L ,   A N D
     M I S C E L L A N E O U S   W R I T I N G S

1 / Independent publications

96   75 Jahre. Idee und Gestaltung Karl Oppermann. Texte
     Günter Gras (sic). Berlin: Meierei C. Bolle, 1956.
97   Die Ballerina. Berlin: Friedenauer Presse, 1963, 2nd.
     edn. 1965. 14 pp.
98   Dich singe ich Demokratie. Neuwied: Luchterhand, 1965;
     rpt. in Über das Selbstverständliche (1968), pp. 7-83
     (Contains: "Es steht zur Wahl," 16 pp; "Ich klage an,"
     13 pp; "Des Kaisers neue Kleider," 14 pp; "Loblied auf
     Willy," 12 pp; "Was ist des Deutschen Vaterland?" 12 pp).
99   Rede über das Selbstverständliche. Neuwied: Luchterhand,
     1965. 14 pp.
100 Der Fall Axel C. Springer am Beispiel Arnold Zweig. Vol-
     taire Flugschriften 15. Berlin: Voltaire, 1967, 76 pp.
101 Briefe über die Grenze: Versuch eines Ost-West-Dialogs
     (with Pavel Kohout). Hamburg: Christian Wegner, 1968,
     118 pp.
102 Über das Selbstverständliche. Neuwied: Luchterhand, 1968.
103 Über meinen Lehrer Döblin und andere Vorträge. Berlin:
     Literarisches Colloquium, 1968.
104 Der Schriftsteller als Bürger--eine Siebenjahresbilanz.
     Ed. Erich Weisbier. Wien: Dr-Karl-Renner-Institut, 1973.
105 Der Bürger und seine Stimme. Reden-Aufsätze-Kommentare.
     Neuwied: Luchterhand, 1974.

2 / Contributions to periodicals, collections and news-
    papers

1956

106 "Die Ballerina." Akzente, 3(1956), 531-39; Berlin:
     Friedenauer Presse, 1963, 2nd. edn. 1965.

1957

107 "Der Inhalt als Widerstand: Bausteine zur Poetik."
     Akzente, 4(1957), 229-35; rpt. Über meinen Lehrer Döblin

(1968), pp. 56-62.

1958

108 "Über das Schreiben von Gedichten." Lyrik unserer Zeit.
Gedichte und Texte, Daten und Hinweise, ed. Horst Wolff
(Dortmund, 1958).

1961

109 "Und was können Schriftsteller tun?" (open letter to Anna
Seghers). Die Zeit, 18 August 1961.
110 "Offener Brief an den Deutschen Schriftstellerverband"
(with Wolfdietrich Schnurre). Die Zeit, 18 August 1961.
111 "Das Gelegenheitsgedicht oder - es ist immer noch, frei
nach Picasso, verboten, mit dem Piloten zu sprechen."
Akzente, 8(1961), 8-11; rpt. Über meinen Lehrer Döblin
(1968), pp. 63-66.
112 "Wer wird dieses Bändchen kaufen?" Die Alternative oder
Brauchen wir eine neue Regierung? ed. Martin Walser (Hamburg: Rowohlt, 1961), pp. 76-80.

1962

113 "Sollte dieser Preis zurückgewiesen werden?" (open letter
to Siegfried Lenz). Die Zeit, 16 February 1962.
114 "Ohrenbeichte: Brief an ein unbeschriebenes Blatt."
Sprache im technischen Zeitalter, 2(1962), 170-71.
115 "Ohrenbeichte." Sprache im technischen Zeitalter, 2
(1962), 341-43.

1964

116 "Kleine Rede für Arno Schmidt." Frankfurter Allgemeine
Zeitung, 19 March 1964; Konkret, No. 4 (1964), pp. 17-18;
rpt. Über meinen Lehrer Döblin (1968), pp. 73-77.
117 "Vor- und Nachgeschichte der Tragödie des Coriolanus von
Livius und Plutarch über Shakespeare bis zu Brecht und
mir." Spandauer Volksblatt (Berlin), 26 April 1964;
Akzente, 11(1964), 194-221; Moderna Språk, 58(1964),
345-67; Club Voltaire, 2(1965), 323-44; rpt. Über meinen
Lehrer Döblin (1968), pp. 27-55.

1965

118 "Offener Brief an Ludwig Erhard." Spandauer Volksblatt
(Berlin), 14 February 1965; rpt. Über das Selbstverständliche (1968), pp. 5-6.
119 "Lieber armer Freund Schlieker." Sprache im technischen
Zeitalter, 5(September 1965).

9

120 "Gesamtdeutscher März." Plädoyer für eine neue Regierung
oder keine Alternative, ed. Hans Werner Richter (Hamburg:
Rowohlt, 1965), p. 18.
121 "Rede über das Selbstverständliche." Süddeutsche Zeitung,
16/17 October 1965; Deutsche Akademie für Sprache und
Dichtung. Darmstadt. Jahrbuch 1965, pp. 92-108; Neuwied:
Berlin: Luchterhand, 1965; Konkret, No. 11 (1966), pp.
6-11; rpt. Über das Selbstverständliche (1968), pp. 84-
104; Büchner-Preis-Reden. 1951-1971. Mit einem Vorwort
von Ernst Johann (Stuttgart: Reclam, 1972).

1966

122 "Willy Brandt und die Friedensenzyklika." Süddeutsche
Zeitung, 11 November 1966.
123 "Von draussen nach drinnen." Der Spiegel, 14(14 November
1966), 170-72; rpt. Literatur im Spiegel, ed. Rolf Becker
(Hamburg: Rowohlt, 1969), pp. 184-87.
124 "An einen jungen Wähler, der sich versucht fühlt, NPD zu
wählen." Berliner Stimme, 26 November 1966; rpt. Über
das Selbstverständliche (1968), pp. 113-19.
125 "Offener Brief an Kurt-Georg Kiesinger." Frankfurter
Allgemeine Zeitung, 1 December 1966; rpt. Über das Selbstverständliche (1968), pp. 125-27.
126 "Offener Briefwechsel mit Willy Brandt." Die Zeit, 2 and
9 December 1966; rpt. Über das Selbstverständliche (1968),
pp. 120-24.
127 "Das Gewissen der SPD." Die Zeit, 9 December 1966; rpt.
Über das Selbstverständliche (1968), pp. 128-31.
128 "Diese neue Regierung. Aber es ist nicht die Zeit für
Resignation und Sentimentalität." Die Zeit, 9 December
1966.
129 "Freundliche Bitte um bessere Feinde" (open letter to
Peter Handke). Sprache im technischen Zeitalter, 20
(1966), Sonderheft 318-20; rpt. Poesie und Politik: Zur
Situation der Literatur in Deutschland, ed. Wolfgang
Kuttenkeuler (Stuttgart: Kohlhammer, 1973), pp. 299-303.
130 "Vom mangelnden Selbstvertrauen der schreibenden Hof-
narren unter Berücksichtigung nicht vorhandener Höfe."
Akzente, 13(1966), 194-99; rpt. Über meinen Lehrer Döblin
(1968), pp. 67-72; rpt. Über das Selbstverständliche
(1968), pp. 105-12.

1967

131 "Über die erste Bürgerpflicht." Die Zeit, 13 January
1967; rpt. Über das Selbstverständliche (1968), pp. 140-
51.
132 "Die melancholische Koalition." Der Monat, 19, No. 220
(January 1967), 9-12; rpt. Über das Selbstverständliche

(1968), pp. 132-39.

133 "Rede von der Gewöhnung." Frankfurter Allgemeine Zeitung, 20 March 1967, pp. 9-10; Tribüne (Frankfurt), 6(1967), 2374-86; rpt. Über das Selbstverständliche (1968), pp. 162-79; rpt. Poesie und Politik: Zur Situation der Literatur in Deutschland, ed. Wolfgang Kuttenkeuler (Stuttgart: Kohlhammer, 1973), pp. 396-403.

134 "Nachruf auf einen Gegner." Stern (Hamburg), 8 May 1967; rpt. Über das Selbstverständliche (1968), pp. 186-90.

135 "Die kommunizierende Mehrzahl. Sollen die Deutschen eine Nation bilden?" Süddeutsche Zeitung, 29 May 1967; rpt. Über das Selbstverständliche (1968), pp. 191-208.

136 "Genau hinsehen. Zum Tod des Bildhauers Karl Hartung." Die Zeit, 4 August 1967.

137 "Über meinen Lehrer Döblin." Akzente, 14(1967), 290-309; rpt. Über meinen Lehrer Döblin (1968), pp. 7-26; rpt. Deutsche Literatur der Gegenwart, ed. Hans Mayer, IV, Bd. 2 (Stuttgart: Goverts, 1972), 481-505; shortened version "Mein Lehrer Döblin," Stuttgarter Zeitung, 26 August 1967.

138 "Offener Brief an Antonin Novotny." Die Zeit, 8 September 1967.

139 "An Pavel Kohout: Briefe." Die Zeit, 22 September 1967; 17 November 1967; 19 January 1968.

1968

140 "Eine Mahnung." Der Abend (Berlin), 8 February 1968.

141 "Briefwechsel mit Klaus Schütz." Der Telegraf (Berlin), 9 March 1968.

142 "Eine Stimme von aussen her." Vorwärts (Bonn), 28 March 1968.

143 "Der Biedersinn gibt wieder den Ton an." Blickpunkt (Berlin), 30 April 1968.

144 "Gewaltätigkeit ist wieder gesellschaftsfähig." Der Spiegel, 22(6 May 1968), 52-58.

145 "Ich bin dabeigewesen." Frankfurter Rundschau, 10 May 1968.

146 "Wir haben nicht die demokratische Reife." Frankfurter Rundschau, 14 May 1968.

147 "Mit vierzig Mark begannen wir ein neues Leben." Der Spiegel, 22(17 June 1968), 60.

148 "Die grosse Koalition ist zum Handeln aufgerufen." Frankfurter Rundschau, 20 June 1968.

149 "Völkermord vor aller Augen. Ein Appell an die Bundesregierung." Die Zeit, No. 41, 1968, p. 5.

150 "Die Prager Lektion." Tschechoslowakei 1968 (Zürich: Arche, 1968), pp. 35-43; rpt. Der Bürger und seine Stimme (1974), pp. 9-13.

151 "Friedenspolitik in Spannungsfeldern." Die Zeit, 22

November 1968.

152 "Über ja und Nein." Die Zeit, 20 December 1968, p. 22;
     rpt. Der Bürger und seine Stimme (1974), pp. 14-20.
153 "Was unterm Strich steht." Stuttgarter Zeitung, 31
     December 1968, p. 39.
154 "Ich bin gegen Radikalkuren." twen, December 1968.
155 "Auschwitz und Treblinka in Afrika." Aufwärts (Köln),
     No. 10, 1968.
156 "Vorwort." Anekdoten um Willy Brandt, ed. Heli Ihlefeld
     (München, Esslingen: Bechtle, 1968).

     1969

157 "Konflikte." Frankfurter Rundschau, 3 February 1969;
     Süddeutsche Zeitung, 3 February 1969; rpt. Der Bürger und
     seine Stimme (1974), pp. 21-26.
158 "Dank studentischer Lethargie." Kölner Stadtanzeiger,
     4 March 1969.
159 "Ein Sieg der Demokratie." Die Neue Gesellschaft, March/
     April 1969.
160 "Günter Grass und die Gewerkschaften. Eine kritische
     Mairede" ("Rede wider die Kurfürsten"). Welt der Arbeit
     (Köln), 16 May 1969; rpt. Der Bürger und seine Stimme
     (1974), pp. 39-45.
161 "Was lesen die Soldaten?" Weser-Kurier (Bremen), 17 May
     1969; Ad lectores (Neuwied: Luchterhand Verlag), No. 9
     (1969), supplement; rpt. Der Bürger und seine Stimme
     (1974), pp. 46-52.
162 "Wer hat Angst vor . . ." dafür (Bonn), No. 1 (May 1969).
163 "Offener Brief an eine CDU-Wählerin." dafür (Bonn), No.
     2(August 1969).
164 "Unser Grundübel ist der Idealismus." Der Spiegel, 23
     (11 August 1969), 94.
165 "Die angelesene Revolution." Der Monat (Berlin), 21, No.
     246 (1969), 34-42; also in: Jens Litten, Eine verpasste
     Revolution? Nachruf auf den SDS (Hamburg, 1969).
166 "Freiheit, ein Wort wie Löffelstiel." In: Günter Grass
     and Paul Schallück, Zwei Reden zur Woche der Brüderlich-
     keit (Köln: Kölnische Gesellschaft für christlich-
     jüdische Zusammenarbeit, 1969); rpt. Der Bürger und seine
     Stimme (1974), pp. 27-38.
167 "Über meinen Verleger." Für Eduard Reifferscheid, ed.
     Elisabeth Borchers (Neuwied: Luchterhand, 1969), pp. 35-
     37.
168 "Die Zukunft der Stückeschreiber." Theater heute, 10
     (1969) Sonderheft, 14.

     1970

169 "Was Erfurt ausserdem bedeutet." Vorwärts (Bonn), 11 May

1970; rpt. Der Bürger und seine Stimme (1974), pp. 73-82.

170 "Schwierigkeiten eines Vaters, seinen Kindern Auschwitz zu erklären." Der Tagesspiegel (Berlin), 27 May 1970; rpt. Der Bürger und seine Stimme (1974), pp. 89-91.

171 "Über das scheintote Theater." Süddeutsche Zeitung, 13/ 14 June 1970.

172 "Zwischen den Terminen." Süddeutsche Zeitung, 3 October 1970; rpt. Der Bürger und seine Stimme (1974), pp. 189-90.

173 "Die eigenen vier Wände." Süddeutsche Zeitung, 17 October 1970; rpt. Der Bürger und seine Stimme (1974), pp. 191-92.

174 "Blindlings." Süddeutsche Zeitung, 31 October 1970; rpt. Der Bürger und seine Stimme (1974), pp. 193-95.

175 "Wie frei wird in Bayern gewählt?" Süddeutsche Zeitung, 14/15 November 1970; rpt. Der Bürger und seine Stimme (1974), pp. 196-98.

176 "Verlorene Provinzen--Gewonnene Einsicht." Süddeutsche Zeitung, 28 November 1970; rpt. Der Bürger und seine Stimme (1974), pp. 199-200.

177 "Betroffen sein." Süddeutsche Zeitung, 12 December 1970; Der Abend (Berlin), 14 December 1970; rpt. Der Bürger und seine Stimme (1974), pp. 201-203.

178 "Bequem auf dem Ast." top (Düsseldorf), No. 12, 1970.

179 "Rede von den begrenzten Möglichkeiten." Club Voltaire. Jahrbuch für kritische Aufklärung. IV, ed. Gerhard Szczesny (Hamburg: Rowohlt, 1970), pp. 145ff; rpt. Der Bürger und seine Stimme (1974), pp. 53-66.

1971

180 "Was nicht vom Himmel fällt." Süddeutsche Zeitung, 2 January 1971; rpt. Der Bürger und seine Stimme (1974), pp. 204-206.

181 "In Ermangelung." Süddeutsche Zeitung, 16 January 1971; rpt. Der Bürger und seine Stimme (1974), pp. 207-209.

182 "In Kreuzberg fehlt ein Minarett." Süddeutsche Zeitung, 30 January 1971; rpt. Der Bürger und seine Stimme (1974), pp. 210-12.

183 "Damals im Mai." Süddeutsche Zeitung, 13 February 1971.

184 "In der Mauser." Süddeutsche Zeitung, 27/28 February 1971; rpt. Der Bürger und seine Stimme (1974), pp. 213-15.

185 "Uhuru heisst Freiheit . . ." Süddeutsche Zeitung, 20/21 March 1971.

186 "Jochen Steffen--meerumschlungen." Der Abend (Berlin), 5 April 1971; Süddeutsche Zeitung, 8/9 April 1971, p. 8.

187 "Teure Umwelt." Süddeutsche Zeitung, 19 April 1971.

188 "Abschlusslisten." Süddeutsche Zeitung, 30 April 1971.

189 "Ein glücklicher Mensch." Süddeutsche Zeitung, 15/16 May 1971.

13

190 "Beim Kappenzählen." Süddeutsche Zeitung, 29/30/31 May 1971.

191 "Der verschämte Siebzehnte." Süddeutsche Zeitung, 26 June 1971; rpt. Der Bürger und seine Stimme (1974), pp. 216-18.

192 "Wie konkret ist 'konkret'?" Süddeutsche Zeitung, 10 July 1971; rpt. Der Bürger und seine Stimme (1974), pp. 219-21.

193 "Die Ehemaligen." Süddeutsche Zeitung, 24/25 July 1971, p. 12; rpt. Der Bürger und seine Stimme (1974), pp. 222-24.

194 "Liegt 'Vorwärts' schon hinter uns?" Süddeutsche Zeitung, 18/19 September 1971, p. 11; rpt. Der Bürger und seine Stimme (1974), pp. 225-27.

195 "Zum Fürchten." Süddeutsche Zeitung, 9/10 October 1971, p. 8; rpt. Der Bürger und seine Stimme (1974), pp. 228-30.

196 "Fussnoten zu einem Preis." Süddeutsche Zeitung, 30 October 1971; rpt. Der Bürger und seine Stimme (1974), pp. 231-33.

197 "Wo sich das Wasser scheidet." Süddeutsche Zeitung, 20 November 1971; rpt. Der Bürger und seine Stimme (1974), pp. 234-36.

198 "Wähler und Gewählte." Süddeutsche Zeitung, 11 December 1971; rpt. Der Bürger und seine Stimme (1974), pp. 237-39.

199 "Begegnungen mit Kohlhaas." Süddeutsche Zeitung, 31 December 1971; rpt. Der Bürger und seine Stimme (1974), pp. 240-42.

200 "Jungbürgerrede: Über Erwachsene und Verwachsene." PEN: Neue Texte deutscher Autoren, ed. Martin Gregor-Dellin (Tübingen, Basel: Horst Erdmann Verlag, 1971), pp. 245-55.

201 "Schriftsteller und Gewerkschaft." Einigkeit der Einzelgänger: Dokumentation des ersten Schriftstellerkongresses des Verbandes deutscher Schriftsteller, ed. Dieter Lattmann (München: Kindler 1971), pp. 25-32; rpt. Der Bürger und seine Stimme (1974), pp. 92-96.

202 "Vorwort." Deutsche Parlamentsdebatten, Bd. III, ed. Eberhard Jäckel (Frankfurt: Fischer Taschenbuch, 1971).

1972

203 "Wiederholter Versuch." Süddeutsche Zeitung, 5 February 1972; rpt. Der Bürger und seine Stimme (1974), pp. 243-45.

204 "Unfehlbar daneben." Süddeutsche Zeitung, 26 February 1972; rpt. Der Bürger und seine Stimme (1974), pp. 246-47.

205 "Ein Alptraum." Süddeutsche Zeitung, 18 March 1972; rpt. Der Bürger und seine Stimme (1974), pp. 248-50.

206 "Oft gefällt sich die Macht in betulicher Sprache" ("Rede gegen die Gewöhnung"). Frankfurter Rundschau, 21 March 1972, p. 12; rpt. Der Bürger und seine Stimme (1974), pp. 135-42.

207 "Die Gier nach der Macht." Süddeutsche Zeitung, 29/30

April, 1 May 1972, p. 11.

208 "Grass appelliert an die Abgeordneten" (open letter to the Bundestag). <u>Frankfurter Rundschau</u>, 13 May 1972, p. 2.

209 "Die Lauen." <u>Süddeutsche Zeitung</u>, 20 May 1972; rpt. <u>Der Bürger und seine Stimme</u> (1974), pp. 251-53.

210 "Angst & Co." <u>Süddeutsche Zeitung</u>, 10 June 1972; rpt. <u>Der Bürger und seine Stimme</u> (1974), pp. 254-56.

211 "Die Deutschen und ihre Dichter." <u>Süddeutsche Zeitung</u>, 1 July 1972; rpt. <u>Der Bürger und seine Stimme</u> (1974), pp. 257-59.

212 "Sie haben den Halt aufgegeben" ("Offener Brief an Karl Schiller"). <u>Frankfurter Rundschau</u>, 7 October 1972, p. 4; rpt. <u>Der Bürger und seine Stimme</u> (1974), pp. 143-45.

213 "Vom Stillstand im Fortschritt: Variationen zu Albrecht Dürers Kupferstich 'Melencolia I'." <u>Am Beispiel Dürers</u>, ed. Hermann Glaser (München: Bruckmann, 1972), pp. 82-97.

214 "Bürger und Politik." <u>Muss Schule "dumm" machen? Plädoyer für eine fortschrittliche Bildungspolitik</u> (Bonn: Sozialdemokratische Wählerinitiative, 1972), pp. 34-38; rpt. <u>Der Bürger und seine Stimme</u> (1974), pp. 130-34.

1973

215 "Die Meinungsfreiheit des Künstlers in unserer Gesellschaft: Eine Rede während des Europarats-Symposiums in Florenz." <u>Frankfurter Rundschau</u>, 30 June 1973, p. VII; rpt. <u>Der Bürger und seine Stimme</u> (1974), pp. 164-72.

216 "Israel und ich." <u>Süddeutsche Zeitung</u>, 31 December 1973; rpt. <u>Der Bürger und seine Stimme</u> (1974), pp. 173-77.

217 "Literatur und Revolution oder des Idyllikers schnaubendes Steckenpferd." <u>Poesie und Politik: Zur Situation der Literatur in Deutschland</u>, ed. Wolfgang Kuttenkeuler (Stuttgart: Kohlhammer, 1973), pp. 341-46; rpt. <u>Der Bürger und seine Stimme</u> (1974), pp. 67-72.

1974

218 "Rückblick auf die Blechtrommel--oder: Der Autor als fragwürdiger Zeuge. Ein Versuch in eigener Sache." <u>Süddeutsche Zeitung</u>, 12/13 January 1974, pp. 99-100.

219 "Versuch eines neuen Dialogs: Günter Grass schreibt einen Offenen Brief über die Grenze an Pavel Kohout." <u>Die Zeit</u>, 15 March 1974, pp. 13-14.

220 "Der lesende Arbeiter." <u>Süddeutsche Zeitung</u>, 5/6 October 1974, pp. 85-86.

221 "Offener Brief an Sinjawskij und Solschenizyn." <u>Frankfurter Rundschau</u>, 10 October 1974; <u>Süddeutsche Zeitung</u>, 10 October 1974, p. 34; <u>Mannheimer Morgen</u>, 11 October 1974, p. 36; <u>Frankfurter Allgemeine Zeitung</u>, 14 October 1974, p. 23.

1975

222   "Exekution eines Autors?" <u>Der Spiegel</u>, 29(12 May 1975),
      158, 161.
223   "Die Legende vom heiligen Lud." <u>Der Tagesspiegel</u>, 21
      September 1975.

V. T H E   W O R K   I N   T R A N S L A T I O N

1 / FICTION

<u>Die Blechtrommel</u>

224   NORWEGIAN: <u>Blikktrommen</u>. Trans. Trygve Greiff. Oslo:
      Gyldendal, 1960.
225   DANISH: <u>Bliktrommen</u>. Trans. Mogens Boisen. Copenhagen:
      Gyldendal, 1961; 2nd. edn. 1968.
226   ENGLISH: <u>The Tin Drum</u>. Trans. Ralph Manheim. London:
      Secker and Warburg, 1961; New York: Random House, 1964;
      New York: Fawcett, 1964; Harmondsworth: Penguin Books,
      1965.
227   FINNISH: <u>Peltirumpu</u>. Trans. Aarno Peromies. Helsinki:
      Otava, 1961; 2nd. edn. 1967.
228   FRENCH: <u>Le tambour</u>. Trans. Jean Amsler. Paris: Editions
      du Seuil, 1961; Paris: Livre de poche, 1969.
229   SWEDISH: <u>Blecktrumman</u>. Trans. Nils Holmberg. Stockholm:
      Bonnier, 1961; 2nd. edn. Stockholm: Aldus/Bonnier, 1964.
230   SERBO-CROATIAN: <u>Dečji doboš</u>. Trans. Olga Trebičnik.
      2 vols. Novi Sad: <u>Bratstvo-jedinstvo</u>, 1963.
231   SPANISH: <u>El tambor de hojalata</u>. Trans. Carlos Gerhard.
      Mexico City: Joaquín Mortiz, 1963.
232   DUTCH: <u>De blikken trommel</u>. Trans. Koos Schuur. Amster-
      dam: Meulenhoff, 1964; 4th. edn. 1969.
233   PORTUGUESE: <u>O Tambor</u>. Trans. Augusto Abelaira. Lisbon:
      Editorial Estúdios Cor, 1964.
234   ITALIAN: <u>Il tamburo di latta</u>. Trans. Lia Secci. Milan:
      Feltrinelli, 1965.
235   JAPANESE: <u>Buriki no taiko</u>. Trans. Takamoto Ken'ichi.
      Tokyo: Shūeisha, 1967.
236   SLOVENIAN: <u>Pločevinasti boben</u>. Trans. Janko Moder.
      Ljubljana: Državna založba Slovenije, 1968.
237   CZECH: <u>Plechový bubínek</u>. Trans. Vladimír Kafka. Prague:
      Mladá fronta, 1969.
238   ROUMANIAN: "Toba de tinichea" (extracts). Trans. Rodica
      Demian and Sânziana Pop. <u>Secolul 20</u>, 9, No. 5(1969),
      53-64.

<u>Katz und Maus</u>

239   FINNISH: <u>Kissa ja hiiri</u>. Trans. Aarno Peromies. Hel-

sinki: Otava, 1962.
240 FRENCH: Le chat et la souris. Trans. Jean Amsler.
Paris: Editions du Seuil, 1962; Lausanne: La Guilde du
Livre, 1966.
241 NORWEGIAN: Katt og mus. Trans. Trygve Greiff. Oslo:
Gyldendal, 1962.
242 SWEDISH: Katt och Råtta. Trans. John W. Walldén. Stockholm: Bonnier, 1962; 2nd. edn. 1967.
243 DANISH: Kat og mus. Trans. Mogens Boisen. Copenhagen:
Gyldendal, 1963; 3rd. edn. 1971.
244 DUTCH: Kat en muis. Trans. Hermien Manger. Amsterdam:
Meulenhoff, 1963; 3rd. edn. 1969.
245 ENGLISH: Cat and Mouse. Trans. Ralph Manheim. New York:
Harcourt, Brace and World; London: Secker and Warburg,
1963; New York: New American Library (Signet), 1964; Harmondsworth: Penguin, 1966.
246 POLISH: Kot i mysz. Trans. Irena Nagonowska and Egon
Naganowski. Warsaw: Czytelnik, 1963.
247 SPANISH: El gato y el ratón. Trans. Carlos Gerhard.
Mexico City: Joaquín Mortiz, 1964.
248 SLOVAK: Mačka a myš. Trans. Perla Bžochová. Bratislava:
Slovenský spisovatel, 1966.
249 ITALIAN: Gatto e topo. Trans. Enrico Filippini. Milan:
Feltrinelli, 1967.
250 CATALAN: El gat i la rata. Trans. Carles Unterlohner.
Barcelona: Edicions 62, 1968.
251 CZECH: Kočka a myš. Trans. Zbyněk Sekal. Prague: Odeon,
1968.
252 HUNGARIAN: Macska és egér. Trans. Elga Sárközy. Budapest: Európa Kiadó, 1968.
253 JAPANESE: Neko to nezumi. Trans. Takamoto Ken'ichi.
Tokyo: Shûeisha, 1968.
254 PORTUGUESE: O gato e o rato. Trans. Carmen Gonzalez.
Lisbon: Europa-América, 1968.
255 ROUMANIAN: "Şoarecele şi pisica." Extracts trans. Rodica
Demian and Sânziana Pop. Secolul 20, 9, No. 5(1969),
25-51.
256 SERBO-CROATIAN: Mačka i miš. Trans. Mira Buljan. Zag-
reb: Zora, 1969.

Hundejahre

257 FINNISH: Koiranvuosia. Trans. Aarno Peromies. Helsinki:
Otava, 1964.
258 DANISH: Hundeår. Trans. Mogens Boisen. Copenhagen:
Gyldendal, 1965.
259 DUTCH: Hondejaren. Trans. Koos Schuur. Amsterdam:
Meulenhoff, 1965; 2nd. edn. 1967.
260 ENGLISH: Dog Years. Trans. Ralph Manheim. New York:
Harcourt, Brace and World; London: Secker and Warburg,

17

1965; New York: Fawcett, 1966; Harmondsworth: Penguin, 1969.

261 FRENCH: Les années de chien. Trans. Jean Amsler. Paris: Editions du Seuil, 1965.

262 NORWEGIAN: Hundeår. Trans. Hans Braarvig. Oslo: Gyldendal, 1965.

263 SERBO-CROATION: Pseće godine. Trans. Ivan Ivanji. Belgrade: Prosveta, 1965.

264 SWEDISH: Hundår. Trans. Lars W. Freij. Stockholm: Bonnier, 1965.

265 ITALIAN: Anni di cani. Trans. Enrico Filippini. Milan: Feltrinelli, 1966.

266 PORTUGUESE: O cão de Hitler. Trans. Lídia de Castro. Lisbon: Editorial Estúdios Cor, 1966.

267 JAPANESE: Inu no toshi. Trans. Nakono Kôji. 2 vols. Tokyo: Shûeisha, 1969.

Örtlich betäubt

268 DUTCH: Plaatselijk verdoofd. Trans. C. Schuur-Kaspers. Amsterdam: Meulenhoff, 1969.

269 ENGLISH: Local Anaesthetic. Trans. Ralph Manheim. New York: Harcourt, Brace and World, 1969; London: Secker and Warburg, 1970; Harmondsworth: Penguin, 1973.

270 SWEDISH: Lokalbedövad. Trans. Ingrid Rüegger and Eva Liljegren. Stockholm: Bonnier, 1970.

271 FRENCH: Anesthésie locale. Trans. Jean Amsler. Paris: Editions du Seuil, 1971.

272 DANISH: Lokalbedøvet. Trans. Mogens Boisen. Copenhagen: Gyldendal, 1971.

273 NORWEGIAN: Lokalbedøvet. Trans. Aksel Bull Njå and Torborg Nedreaas. Oslo: Gyldendal, 1971.

Aus dem Tagebuch einer Schnecke

274 ENGLISH: From the Diary of a Snail. Trans. Ralph Manheim. New York: Harcourt, Brace Jovanovich, 1973; London: Secker and Warburg, 1974.

Miscellaneous fiction

275 ENGLISH: "The Escalator." Trans. Tim Nater and Robie Macauley. Playboy, 20(December 1973), 213.

276 ENGLISH: "The meadow" ("Meine grüne Wiese"). Trans. Patrick O'Neill. Anvil (Dublin), 1975, pp. 45-49.

2 / DRAMA

Collections

277 ENGLISH: Four Plays: Flood. Mister, mister. Only Ten

Minutes to Buffalo. The Wicked Cooks. Trans. Ralph Manheim and A. Leslie Willson. Introduced by Martin Esslin. New York: Harcourt, Brace and World, 1967; London: Secker and Warburg, 1968; Harmondsworth: Penguin Books, 1972.

278 ITALIAN: Tutto il teatro: I plebei provano la rivolta. Acqua alta. A dieci minuti da Buffalo. Una discussione pubblica. Trans. Enrico Filippini. Milan: Feltrinelli, 1968.

279 FRENCH: Théâtre. Trans. Jean Amsler. Paris: Editions du Seuil, 1973 (Contains: Tonton, Les méchants cuisiniers, La crue, A dix minutes de Buffalo).

Onkel, Onkel

280 ENGLISH: "Mister, mister." Trans. Ralph Manheim. Four Plays. New York: Harcourt, Brace and World, 1967.

Beritten hin und zurück

281 ENGLISH: "Rocking back and forth." Trans. Michael Benedikt and Joseph Goradza. Postwar German Theatre, ed. and trans. Michael Benedikt and George E. Wellwarth (New York: E.P. Dutton, 1967), pp. 261-75.

"Noch zehn Minuten bis Buffalo"

282 TURKISH: On dakka sonra Buffalo. Trans. Adalet Cimcoz. Istanbul: Istanbul Matbaasi, 1964.

283 ENGLISH: "Only Ten Minutes to Buffalo." Trans. Ralph Manheim. Four Plays. New York: Harcourt, Brace and World, 1967.

284 ENGLISH: "The Salt Lake Line." Trans. Christopher Holme. German Writing Today, ed. Christopher Middleton (Baltimore: Penguin Books, 1967), pp. 61-78.

Hochwasser

285 ENGLISH: "Flood." Trans. Ralph Manheim. Four Plays. New York: Harcourt, Brace and World, 1967.

286 CZECH: "Povodeň." Západoněmecké moderní drama, trans. Jitka Bodláková and Jiří Stach (Prague: Orbis, 1969).

"Die bösen Köche"

287 ENGLISH: "The Wicked Cooks." Trans. James L. Rosenberg. The New Theatre of Europe, ed. Robert W. Corrigan, Vol. 2(New York: Dell, 1964), pp. 115-76.

288 CZECH: Zlí kuchaři. Trans. Jan Tomek. Prague: Dilia, 1967.

289 ENGLISH: "The Wicked Cooks." Trans. A. Leslie Willson.

<u>Four Plays</u>. New York: Harcourt, Brace and World, 1967.

<u>Die Plebejer proben den Aufstand</u>

290 ENGLISH: <u>The Plebeians Rehearse the Uprising</u>. Trans.
Ralph Manheim. New York: Harcourt, Brace and World, 1966;
London: Secker and Warburg, 1967; Harmondsworth: Penguin,
1972.
291 SWEDISH: <u>Plebejerna repeterar upproret</u>. Trans. Per E.
Wahlund. Stockholm: Bonnier, 1967.
292 FRENCH: <u>Les plébéiens répètent l'insurrection</u>. Trans.
Jean Amsler. Paris: Editions du Seuil, 1968.
293 SPANISH: <u>Los plebeyos ensayan la rebelión</u>. Trans.
Heleno Saña Alcón. Madrid: Edicusa, 1969.

<u>Davor</u>

294 ENGLISH: "Uptight." Trans. A. Leslie Willson. <u>Dimen-
sion</u>, Special Issue, 1970, pp. 91-122 (Only scenes 1, 3,
5, 6).
295 ENGLISH: <u>Max: A play by Günter Grass</u>. Trans. A. Leslie
Willson and Ralph Manheim. New York: Harcourt Brace
Jovanovich, 1972.

3 / POETRY

<u>Die Vorzüge der Windhühner</u>

296 ENGLISH: "Open Wardrobe." Trans. Michael Hamburger.
<u>Poetry</u>, 98(June 1961), 154.
297 ENGLISH: "Midge Plague." Trans. Christopher Middleton.
<u>Times Literary Supplement</u>, 27 September 1963, p. 732.
298 ENGLISH: "The school for tenors. Open wardrobe. Preven-
tion of cruelty to animals." Trans. Michael Hamburger.
<u>Modern German Poetry</u>, ed. Michael Hamburger and Christo-
pher Middleton (New York: Grove Press, 1962), pp. 368-71.
299 ENGLISH: "Unsuccessful raid. Family matters." Trans.
Michael Hamburger. <u>Evergreen Review</u>, No. 36(June 1965),
93.
300 SPANISH: "La comida de los profetas." <u>Humboldt</u>, 7, No.
25(1966), 111.
301 ENGLISH: "Fight." Trans. Kenneth Hughes. <u>The Literary
Review</u>, 17(1974), 540-41.

<u>Gleisdreieck</u>

302 ENGLISH: "Transformation." Trans. Michael Hamburger.
<u>Times Literary Supplement</u>, 13 October 1961, p. 725; rpt.
<u>Modern German Poetry</u>, ed. Michael Hamburger and Christo-

pher Middleton (New York: Grove Press, 1962), pp. 372-73.

303 ENGLISH: "Crack-up. In the egg. Frost and bite. The ballad of the black cloud. To all the gardeners." Trans. Jerome Rothenberg. Evergreen Review, 32(April-May 1964), 67-69.

304 FRENCH: "Chanson d'enfant." Trans. Paul Mayer. Lettres Nouvelles, December 1965/January 1966, p. 231.

305 ENGLISH: Selected Poems. Trans. Michael Hamburger and Christopher Middleton. New York: Harcourt, Brace, and World; London: Secker and Warburg, 1966 (Selected poems from Die Vorzüge der Windhühner and Gleisdreieck).

306 ENGLISH: "The ballad of the black cloud." Trans. Elizabeth G. Lord. The Literary Review, 17(1974), 539-40.

307 ENGLISH: "Annabel Lee: Hommage à E.A. Poe." Trans. Sharon Edwards Jackiw. The Literary Review, 17(1974), 541.

Ausgefragt

308 ENGLISH: New Poems. Trans. Michael Hamburger. New York: Harcourt, Brace, and World, 1968 (Selected poems from Ausgefragt).

309 ENGLISH: Poems of Günter Grass. Trans. Michael Hamburger and Christopher Middleton. Introduction by Michael Hamburger. Harmondsworth: Penguin Books, 1969 (A combined edition of Selected Poems and New Poems).

310 HUNGARIAN: Vallató. Trans. Balázs Boldog et al. Budapest: Európa Kiadó, 1969.

Mariazuehren

311 ENGLISH: Inmarypraise. Trans. Christopher Middleton. New York: Harcourt Brace Jovanovich, 1974.

Liebe geprüft

312 ENGLISH: Love tested. Trans. Michael Hamburger. New York: Harcourt Brace Jovanovich, 1975 (Limited edition of 25 copies).

4 / THEORETICAL, POLITICAL, AND MISCELLANEOUS WRITINGS

Briefe über die Grenze

313 ENGLISH: "Open letter to Pavel Kohout." Trans. anon. Atlas, 14(November 1967), 54-55.

314 FRENCH: Lettres par-dessus la frontière. Trans. Richard Dentruck. Paris: C. Bourgois, 1969.

Über das Selbstverständliche

315 FRENCH: "Discours de remerciement." Trans. Bernard
Lortholary. Lettres Nouvelles, December 1965/January
1966, pp. 316-35.
316 ENGLISH: "On the lack of self-confidence of the literary
court jester without a court." Trans. Kimberly Sparks.
American German Review, 32, No. 5(1966), 20-22.
317 ENGLISH: "Günter Grass's Open Letter to Kurt Kiesinger."
Trans. anon. Nation, 204(13 February 1967), 214.
318 ENGLISH: Speak Out! Speeches, Open Letters, Commentar-
ies. Trans. Ralph Manheim and others. New York: Harcourt, Brace and World; London: Secker and Warburg, 1969.
319 FRENCH: Evidences politiques. Trans. Jean Amsler, Luc
de Goustine, and Bernard Lortholary. Paris: Editions du
Seuil, 1969.
320 JAPANESE: Jimei no koto ni tsuite. Trans. Takamoto
Ken'ichi and Miyahara Akira. Tokyo: Shûeisha, 1970.

Über meinen Lehrer Döblin

321 FRENCH: "Le Coriolan de Shakespeare et de Brecht."
Trans. anon. Preuves, No. 164(October 1964), pp. 3-16.
322 FRENCH: "La poésie de circonstance." Trans. Paul Mayer.
Lettres Nouvelles, December 1965/January 1966, pp. 227-30.
323 SPANISH: "Sobre mi maestro Döblin." Trans. Ramón de
Haro. Humboldt, 9, No. 34(1968), 71-77.

Der Bürger und seine Stimme

324 FRENCH: "La leçon de Prague." Trans. anon. Preuves,
No. 215/216(February/March 1969), pp. 64-67.

VI. INTERVIEWS

1959

325 Kirn, Richard. "Sein Zwerg haut auf die Trommel." Frankfurter Neue Presse, 14 November 1959, p. 36.

1960

326 Loetscher, Hugo. "Günter Grass." Du (Zürich), 20, No.
6(1960), 15-20; rpt. Gert Loschütz, Von Buch zu Buch,
pp. 190-96.

1961

327 "Lyric heute" (discussion). Akzente, 8(1961), 38-54.

1962

328 Bourrée, Manfred. "Das Okular des Günter Grass." Echo
der Zeit (Recklinghausen), 18 November 1962; rpt. Gert
Loschütz, Von Buch zu Buch, pp. 196-202.

1963

329 Baroth, Hans Dieter. "Das Ärgernis Grass." Westfälische
Rundschau (Dortmund), 1 September 1963.
330 Serke, Jürgen. "pornographie und blasphemie sind keine
literarischen begriffe. ein gespräch mit Günter Grass--
andrej Wadja verfilmt die novelle 'Katz und Maus.'" upi,
14 October 1963.
331 Anon. "Bild eines Bestsellerautors." Bonner Generalanzeiger, 18 October 1963.
332 Anon. "Schulklassengespräch mit Günter Grass am 10.12.
1963." Wie stehen Sie dazu? Jugend fragt Prominente, ed.
Manfred Grunert and Barbara Grunert (München, Bern, 1967),
pp. 74-86.
333 Hasenclever, Walter. "Writers in Berlin: A Three-way
Discussion." Atlantic Monthly, 212 (December 1963), 110-
13.

1964

334 Bauke, J.P. "A talk with Günter Grass." New York Times
Book Review, 69(31 May 1964), 16.
335 Vormweg, Heinrich. "Der Berühmte." Magnum (Köln),
Jahresheft 1964; rpt. Gert Loschütz, Von Buch zu Buch,
pp. 202-207.

1965

336 Anon. "Conversation with Simonov. With Günter Grass and
Uwe Johnson." Encounter, 24(January 1965), 88-91.
337 Morlock, Martin. "Die schmutzigen Finger." Der Spiegel,
19 (31 March 1965), 145.
338 Beichmann, Arnold. "Meet Günter Grass." Christian
Science Monitor, 27 May 1965, p. 7.
339 Anon. "Ich will auch der SPD einiges zumuten." Der
Spiegel, 19(15 September 1965), 70-72.

1966

340 Gaus, Günter. "Manche Freundschaft zerbrach am Ruhm."
Zur Person: Portraits in Frage und Antwort, Bd. 2 (München: Feder, 1966), pp. 110-22.
341 Hoffmann, Jens. "Ein Staat ist noch kein Vaterland: Die
Schriftsteller und der dritte Weg--ein Gespräch mit Günter

23

Grass." <u>Christ und Welt</u>, 11 February 1966, p. 19.

342 Anon. "Grass speaks." <u>Atlas</u>, 11(April 1966), 250.

243 Botsford, Keith. "Günter Grass is a different drummer."
<u>New York Times Magazine</u>, 8 May 1966, pp. 28ff.

344 Anon. "Günter Grass-Interview." <u>Retorte</u> (Ludwigshafen),
December 1966.

345 Leiser, Erwin. "Gespräch über Deutschland." <u>Die Welt-
woche</u> (Zürich), 23 December 1966; rpt. Gert Loschütz, <u>Von
Buch zu Buch</u>, pp. 207-10.

346 vis. "Das Silvester WAZ-Gespräch." <u>Westdeutsche Allge-
meine</u> (Gelsenkirchen), 31 December 1966.

1967

347 Hartlaub, Geno. "Wir, die wir übriggeblieben sind . . ."
<u>Sonntagsblatt</u> (Hamburg), 1 January 1967; rpt. Gert Lo-
schütz, <u>Von Buch zu Buch</u>, pp. 211-16.

348 Anon. "Galerie der Buhmänner: Gespräch mit Günter Grass."
<u>Kontraste</u> (Freiburg), January/February 1967.

349 Kotschenreuther, Hellmuth. "Politik nicht vom Olymp herab:
Der Autor berichtet von seinen Eindrücken in Israel." <u>NRZ</u>
(Essen), 8 April 1967.

350 Drenhaus, Heinz. "Sind die Deutschen keine Nation? Ein
Dialog mit Günter Grass." <u>Vorwärts</u> (Bad Godesberg), 6
July 1967.

351 Zimmer, Dieter E. "Politik interessiert zu Zeit mehr.
Ein Interview mit Günter Grass." <u>Die Zeit</u>, 27 October
1967, p. 17.

352 Marbach, Renate. "Keine Scheu vor Meinungsstreit. Die
NS-Spielart des Faschismus hat ja nicht mit Auschwitz an-
gefangen." <u>Stuttgarter Nachrichten</u>, 31 October 1967.

353 Anon. "Grass-Interview." <u>Die Glocke</u> (Hannover), December
1967.

354 <u>Deutschlandgespräche</u>. With Hans Werner Richter, Rudolf
Augstein et al. München: Hase und Koehler, 1967.

1968

355 Zimmer, Dieter. "Interview with Günter Grass: Revolution
(and Libel) on the German Left." <u>Encounter</u>, 30 (January
1968), 71-74.

356 Rieck, Horst. "Protest ohne Instinkte: AZ-Interview mit
Günter Grass zur politischen Situation." <u>Abendzeitung /
8-Uhr-Blatt</u> (München), 20 June 1968.

357 Höfer, Werner. "Nicht hinter Utopien herjagen." <u>Die
Zeit</u>, 28 June 1968.

358 Anon. "Grass empfiehlt Prager Modell. Auszüge aus dem
Interview, das Günter Grass am 27. Juni 1968 dem Jugend-
funk von 'Radio Prag' gegeben hat." <u>Süddeutsche Zeitung</u>,
29 June 1968.

24

359 Anon. "Der Geist Stalins über Prag." Abendzeitung/8-Uhr-Blatt (München), 22 August 1968.

360 Giegold, Heinrich. "Der unbequeme, offene Günter Grass." Frankenpost (Hof), 24 December 1968.

1969

361 B., C.v. "Das Establishment braucht Provokation." Abendzeitung/8-Uhr-Blatt (München), 4 February 1969.

362 u. "Ich kenne das Rezept auch nicht. Gespräch mit Günter Grass." Wiesbadener Kurier, 4 February 1969.

363 Schäble, Günter. "Die Ideologien haben versagt. Interview der Stuttgarter Zeitung mit Günter Grass." Stuttgarter Zeitung, 18 February 1969, p. 3.

364 Stiller, Klaus. "Man kann nicht bei der Nein-Position stehenbleiben." Frankfurter Rundschau, 10 March 1969.

365 Anon. "Günter Grass zu seinem Misserfolg." Stuttgarter Nachrichten, 10 March 1969.

366 Bauer, Heinrich. "Ein Goethe für unsere Tage." Donau-Kurier, 15 March 1969.

367 Ihlau, Olaf. "Grass: Die Studenten vor dem Verschleiss durch den SDS retten." NRZ (Essen), 29 March 1969.

368 Lorenzen, Rudolf. "Manipulation verboten." Berliner Leben, No. 3, 1969.

369 Rischbieter, Henning. "Gespräch mit Günter Grass." Theater heute, 10, No. 4(1969), 31-34.

370 Krauss, Erika. "Kiesinger und Beate--ein schönes Paar." Hamburger Morgenpost, 25 April 1969.

371 Häsler. "Gespräch mit Günter Grass." ex libris (Zürich), No. 5, 1969, pp. 11-25.

372 Offenbach, Jürgen. "Ich bin doch kein Bürgerschreck. Der Schriftsteller glaubt: Nur die SPD garantiert Reformen." Stuttgarter Nachrichten, 24 May 1969.

373 Röllinghof, Manfred. "Die NPD ist nur die Spitze eines Eisbergs." Main-Echo (Aschaffenburg), 29 May 1969.

374 Reiser, Hans. "Was ich wirklich gesagt habe. Der Schriftsteller nimmt Stellung zu den Vorwürfen der CSU, er habe im amerikanischen Fernsehen Bundeskanzler Kiesinger beschimpft." Süddeutsche Zeitung, 11 June 1969.

375 Anon. "Grass: Wähler braucht nicht unbedingt ein Parteibuch." Hannoversche Presse, 24 July 1969.

376 Weitz, Werner. "Nie gegen das christliche Ethos. Fragen an den Autor Günter Grass." Würzburger Katholisches Sonntagsblatt, 27 July 1969.

377 Anon. "Der Wähler soll mitbestimmen." Hamburger Morgenpost, 30 August 1969.

378 Anon. "Ich bleibe bei Hosen." Epoca (München), No. 10, 1969.

379 Anon. "Grass: Wenn es nicht klappt--dann Opposition. Wer regiert mit wem?" Abendzeitung/8-Uhr-Blatt (München), 1 October 1969.

380 Klunker, H. "Günter Grass: Ich und meine Rollen--Ein Gespräch." Sonntagsblatt, 12 October 1969, p. 25.
381 Lebeer, Irmelin. "Günter Grass: Pour l'écrivain, s'engager signifie travailler." La quinzaine littéraire (Paris), 15 October 1969.
382 Linke, Rainer. "Wer kennt schon Günter Grass." Realist (Augsburg), No. 11, 1969.
383 Bayer, Hans. "Vielleicht ein politisches Tagebuch. Der Autor der Blechtrommel äussert sich über seinen Standort nach dem Wahlkampf." Stuttgarter Nachrichten, 21 November 1969.
384 Flach, Karl-Hermann. "Das ist nicht nur eine griechische Affäre. Die Militärdiktatur in Athen geht alle Europäer an." Frankfurter Rundschau, 10 December 1969.
385 Roos, Peter. "Günter-Grass-Interview." blechmusik (Würzburg), No. 12, 1969.

1970

386 Toeppen, Hans. "Hundejahre für die Berliner Schule? Ein Interview mit Günter Grass zum Rücktritt von Senator Evers." Tagesspiegel (Berlin), 6 March 1970.
387 Berger, David. "An encounter with Günter Grass." American German Review, 36, No. 4(1970), 18-19.
388 Riehl, Hans. "Ein langer Marsch." tz (München), 14 May 1970.
389 Engert, Jürgen. "Ich bin zu realistisch." Christ und Welt (Stuttgart), 3 July 1970.
390 Hayman, Ronald. "Two Interviews: 2. Günter Grass." Encounter (London), 35 (September 1970), 26-29.
391 Loy, Leo. "Nicht besonders gelungen. SPD-Wahlkämpfer in Nürnberg." Abendzeitung/8-Uhr-Blatt (München), 2 November 1970.
392 Anon. "Können die Schriftsteller streiken? Spiegel-Gespräch mit Dieter Lattmann und Günter Grass über den Autoren-Verband." Der Spiegel, 24 (16 November 1970), 241-45.
393 Fliscar, Fritz. "Input-Interview." input, No. 12, 1970.

1971

394 Luuk, Ernst, and Jürgen Brinckmeyer. "Der fundamentale Unterschied zwischen Sozialdemokratie und Kommunismus sollte Sozialdemokraten bewusst sein. Kein Punkt Null in der Geschichte." Berliner Stimme, 27 February 1971.
395 Bauer, Leo. "Ich bin Sozialdemokrat, weil ich ohne Furcht leben will. Gespräch mit Günter Grass." Die Neue Gesellschaft (Bad Godesberg), No. 2, 1971; rpt. Der Bürger und seine Stimme (1974), pp. 97-114.
396 Tank, Kurt Lothar. "Die Parolen und die Produktion: Ein

Gespräch mit Günter Grass." <u>Sonntagsblatt</u>, 25 July 1971, p. 21.

397 Arnold, Heinz Ludwig. "Ein Gespräch mit Günter Grass." <u>Text + Kritik</u>, No. 1/1a, 4th edn. (1971), pp. 1-26.

398 Weber, Gerhard. "Die Resignation des Günter Grass." <u>Der Literat</u>, 13(1971), 43.

399 Rudolph, Ekkehardt (ed.). "Günter Grass." <u>Protokoll zur Person: Autoren über sich und ihr Werk</u> (München: List, 1971), pp. 59-72.

1972

400 Mathiopoulos, Basil P. "'Keine Konzessionen bei dem, was ich sagen will': Interview mit dem Schriftsteller Grass vor seiner Reise nach Griechenland." <u>Frankfurter Rundschau</u>, 20 March 1972, p. 3.

401 Moskin, J. Robert. "Günter Grass and the murderer at the desk." <u>Intellectual Digest</u> (Boulder, Colo.), April 1972, pp. 19-22.

402 Terry, Antony. "The bloody Olympics in Munich--a German speaks out." <u>Sunday Times</u>, 17 September 1972.

403 Gössmann, Wilhelm. "Günter Grass: Interview am 8. Juni 1972." <u>Geständnisse: Heine im Bewusstsein heutiger Autoren</u>, ed. Wilhelm Gössmann (Düsseldorf: Droste Verlag, 1972), pp. 174-78.

404 Simmerding, Gertrud, and Christof Schmid. <u>Literarische Werkstatt: Interviews</u>. München: Oldenbourg, 1972.

405 Bronnen, Barbara. "Schnecke ohne Schneckenhaus: Ein Interview mit Günter Grass." <u>Publikation</u> (München), 22(1972), 38-40.

1973

406 Anon. "Pressegespräch mit Günter Grass am 23. Februar 1973." <u>Der Schriftsteller als Bürger--eine Siebenjahresbilanz</u>, ed. Erich Weisbier (Wien: Dr-Karl-Renner-Institut, 1973), pp. 35-61.

407 Heinemann, Frank J. "Günter Grass sieht lauter kleine Metterniche." <u>Stuttgarter Zeitung</u>, 6 September 1973, p. 3.

408 Engert, Jürgen. "Günter Grass pflegt hellgraue Skepsis." <u>Deutsche Zeitung</u>, 7 September 1973, p. 36.

409 Schwarz, Wilhelm Johannes. "Auf Wahlreise mit Günter Grass." <u>Grass: Kritik-Thesen-Analysen</u>, ed. Manfred Jurgensen (Bern: Francke, 1973), pp. 151-65.

1974

410 Lerchbacher, Hans. "Viele Gründe für den Kanzlersturz." <u>Frankfurter Rundschau</u>, 9 May 1974.

411 Anon. "Das ist schon der Stil der Springer-Presse." <u>Frankfurter Rundschau</u>, 16 October 1974.

1975

412 Göpfert, Peter Hans. "Der Mann mit der Schnecke im Auge." Stuttgarter Nachrichten, 10 March 1975, p. 8.
413 Arnold, Heinz Ludwig. "Verändert der Ruhm den Autor?" Die Tat (Zürich), 22 March 1975, p. 22.
414 Göpfert, Peter Hans. "Das ironische Semikolon." Rhein-Neckar-Zeitung, 22 March 1975.
415 Göpfert, Peter Hans. "Bayrische Schuhe und anderes." Die Presse, 25 March 1975.
416 Matthiesen, Hayo. "Pädagogik kann nicht alles: Günter Grass über Deutschunterricht und Gesamtschule, Bildungs-jargon, Elternproteste und Beamtenstreik." Die Zeit, 7 November 1975, p. 15.

SECONDARY

I. BIBLIOGRAPHICAL

1 / Bibliographies

500 Wieser, Theodor. "Bibliographie." Günter Grass. Porträt und Poesie (Neuwied, Berlin: Luchterhand, 1968), pp.
161-174.
501 Loschütz, Gert. "Literaturhinweise." Von Buch zu Buch
(1968), pp. 226-32.
502 Schwarz, Wilhelm Johannes. "Bibliographie." Der Erzähler Günter Grass (Bern, München: Francke, 1969), pp.
133-48.
503 Blomster, W.V. "Bibliography." In: Kurt Lothar Tank,
Günter Grass, trans. John Conway (New York: Frederick Ungar, 1969), pp. 117-27.
504 Church, Margaret, with Ronald Cummings and Charles Whit-
aker. "Five modern German novelists: A bibliography
(1960-1970)." Modern Fiction Studies, 17(1971), 139-56
(Günter Grass: 140-41).
505 Görtz, Franz Josef. "Kommentierte Auswahl-Bibliographie."
Text + Kritik, No. 1/1a, 4. Aufl. 1971, pp. 97-113.
506 Kaufmann, Gertrude, and Franz Josef Görtz. "Bibliographie." Günter Grass--Dokumente zur politischen Wirkung,
hrsg. Heinz Ludwig Arnold und Franz Josef Görtz (Stuttgart: Richard Boorberg, 1971), pp. 406-15.
507 Woods, Jean M. "Günter Grass: a selected bibliography.
Part I." West Coast Review, 5, No. 3 (January 1971),
52-56.
508 Woods, Jean. "Bibliography: Günter Grass, part II."
West Coast Review, 6, No. 1(June 1971), 31-40.
509 Pownall, David E. Articles on twentieth century literature: an annotated bibliography 1954-1970 (New York:
Kraus-Thomson, 1973), pp. 1330-36.
510 Everett, George A. A Select Bibliography of Günter Grass
(From 1956 to 1973). New York: Burt Franklin, 1974.

2 / Surveys of criticism

511 Arnold, Heinz Ludwig. "Grass-Kritiker." Text + Kritik,
No. 1(1964), 17-21.
512 Loschütz, Gert (ed.). Von Buch zu Buch--Günter Grass in
der Kritik: Eine Dokumentation. Neuwied, Berlin: Luchterhand, 1968.

29

513 Grathoff, Dirk. "Schnittpunkte von Literatur und Politik. Günter Grass und die neuere deutsche Grass-Rezeption." Basis, 1(1970), 134-52.

514 Görtz, Franz Josef. "Günter Grass und die Kritik: Ein Panorama." Text + Kritik, No. 1/1a, 4. Aufl. (1971), pp. 85-96.

515 Arnold, Heinz Ludwig, and Franz Josef Görtz, eds. Günter Grass--Dokumente zur politischen Wirkung. Stuttgart: Richard Boorberg, 1971.

516 Eichmann, Waldemar. "The critical reception of Günter Grass in France from 1961-1971." Diss. University of Arkansas, 1973. Dissertation Abstracts International, 34 (1973), 2620-A.

3 / Journal issues devoted to Günter Grass

517 Dimension, Special Issue 1970.

518 Modern Fiction Studies, 17, No. 1 (Spring 1971). Special Number: The modern German Novel. Günter Grass: pp. 43-77.

519 Text + Kritik (Göttingen), No. 1(1964); 4th. edn. (No. 1/1a) 1971.

II. GENERAL

1955

520 Hornung, Peter. "Die Gruppe, die keine Gruppe ist." Tages-Anzeiger (Regensburg), May 1955.

1960

521 Geerdts, Hans Jürgen, Peter Gugisch, Gerhard Kasper, Rudolf Schmidt. "Zur Problematik der kritisch-oppositio-nellen Literatur in Westdeutschland (H. E. Nossack, G. Grass, Chr. Geissler, P. Schallück)." Wissenschaftliche Zeitschrift der Ernst-Moritz-Arndt-Universität Greifswald, 9(1960), 357-68.

522 Heissenbüttel, Helmut. "Und es kam Uwe Johnson." Deutsche Zeitung (Köln), 10 November 1960.

1961

523 Anon. "Ost-Kongress." Der Spiegel, 15(7 June 1961), 68.

524 Böhm, Anton. "Ärger mit Günter Grass." Wort und Wahrheit (Freiburg i. Br.), 16(1961), 407-408.

525 Grau, Werner. "Günter Grass." Der Jungbuchhandel, 15 (1961), 466-67.

526 Günzel, Manfred. "Der Blechtrommler." Blätter und Bilder, No. 12(1961), 79.
527 Petit, Henri. "Günter Grass." Parisien libéré, 31 October 1961.
528 Walkó, György. "Günter Grass és a botránkozok." Nagyvilág (Budapest), 6, No. 6(1961), 825-27.
529 Zielinski, Hans. "Die unbequemen Fragen des Günter Grass." Die Welt, 30 May 1961.

1962

530 Anon. "Grass Kritik: Wallerands Weh." Der Spiegel, 16 (28 February 1962), 68-70.
531 Anon. "Richters Richtfest." Der Spiegel, 16(24 October 1962), 91-106.
532 Anon. "Grass ist ein kalter Krieger, Böll ein Verleumder." SBZ-Archiv (Köln), 13, No. 17(1962), 272.
533 Wallerand, Theodor. "Günter Grass. Ein Danziger Schriftsteller?" Unser Danzig, 14, No. 3(1962), 8.

1963

534 Anon. "Grass: Zunge heraus." Der Spiegel, 17(4 September 1963), 64-69, 72-78.
535 Fehse, Willi. "Günter Grass." Von Goethe bis Grass: Biografische Porträts zur Literatur (Bielefeld: Gieseking, 1963), pp. 227-31.
536 Klicker, J.R. "Grass muss über Hansmann wachsen." Ansätze (Stuttgart), No. 34(1963), pp. 22-23.
537 Spelman, Franz. "Günter Grass: a big new talent." Show, 3 (January 1963), 85.
538 Wagenbach, Klaus. "Marginalie." Bayrischer Rundfunk (München), 29 March 1963; rpt. Gert Loschütz, Von Buch zu Buch, pp. 101-103.
539 Wagenbach, Klaus. "Günter Grass." Schriftsteller der Gegenwart, ed. Klaus Nonnenmann (Olten, Freiburg i. Br.: Walter, 1963), pp. 118-26.
540 Zatonskij, D.V. "Priëm i metod." Voprosy Literatury (Moscow), 7, No. 4(April 1963), 162-77.

1964

541 Anon. "Names from abroad 7: Günter Grass." Times, 30 April 1964, p. 17.
542 Ahl, Herbert. "Ohne Scham--ohne Tendenz--ohne Devise: Günter Grass." Literarische Portraits (München, Wien: Albert Langen Georg Müller, 1962-64), pp. 28-35.
543 Bodláková, Jitka. "Günter Grass." Divadlo (Prague), No. 2(February 1964), pp. 50-54.
544 Krüger, Horst. "Literatur und Prominenz." Der Literat, 7, No. 9(1964), 97-98.

545 Leonhardt, Rudolf. "The nightmare fairy-tales of Günter Grass." Manchester Guardian, 16 January 1964, p. 6.

546 Röhl, Klaus Rainer. "Grass in Weimar. Zur Tagung der Weimarer Akademie am 20-22. November." Konkret, No. 12 (December 1964), pp. 30-31.

547 Rühmkorf, Peter. "Erkenne die Marktlage!" Sprache im technischen Zeitalter, 3(1963/64), 781-84.

548 Wintzen, René. "Günter Grass le Non-Conformist." Documents (Paris), March-April 1964; trans. Gert Loschütz, Von Buch zu Buch, pp. 104-10.

1965

549 Anon. "Grass takes to the Stump." America, 113(24 July 1965), 89.

550 Anon. "Keeping off the Grass." Times Literary Supplement, 64 (30 September 1965), 859-60.

551 Beck, Michael. "Der umgekehrte Trommler. Günter Grass-- Schwarzer Koch aus Danzig." Gemeinschaft und Politik (Bad Godesberg), 13, No. 5/6 (1965), 177-79.

552 Beer, K.W. "Grass und die Folgen. Die 'Formulierungs- helfer' der SPD." Die politische Meinung, No. 108(1965), pp. 8-11.

553 Edschmid, Kasimir. "Rede auf den Preisträger." Deutsche Akademie für Sprache und Dichtung. Jahrbuch, 1965, pp. 82-91.

554 Figes, Eva. "Grass roots." Manchester Guardian, 12 November 1965, p. 11.

555 Frisch, Max. "Grass als Redner." Die Zeit, 24 September 1965, p. 16.

556 Gittleman, Sol. "Guenter Grass: Notes on the Theology of the Absurd." Crane Review, 8(1965), 32-35.

557 Gombrowicz, Witold. "Dziennik transatlantycki." Kultura (Paris), No. 1/207-2/208 (1965), pp. 3-10.

558 Hoffmann, Jens. "Laudatio auf ein Ärgernis. Günter Grass und der Georg-Büchner-Preis." Christ und Welt, 15 October 1965, p. 25.

559 Horst, Karl August. "Grass, Günter." Handbuch der deutschen Gegenwartsliteratur, ed. Hermann Kunisch (München: Nymphenburg, 1965), pp. 216-17; 2nd. rev edn. 1969, Vol. I, pp. 238-41.

560 Kahler, Erich v. "Form und Entformung." Merkur, 19 (1965), 318-35, 413-28.

561 Kellen, Konrad. "Grass and Johnson in New York." American German Review, 31 (June-July 1965), 35-37.

562 Lattmann, Dieter. "Geborgte Vergangenheit--verspätete Gegenwart. Wie jung sind junge deutsche Autoren?" Die Welt, 23 December 1965, p. 751.

563 Reich-Ranicki, Marcel. "Hüben und drüben. Goes, Grass, und Weiss." Die Zeit, 19 March 1965, p. 23.

564 Scherman, David E. "Green Years for Grass." Life, 58

(4 June '65), 51-56.
565 Schmidt, Josef H.K. "Günter Grass: Artistische Langsam-
keit, Literarische Matinée." Neue Zürcher Nachrichten,
30 November 1965.
566 Schönfelder, Fritz. "Fünf Variationen über ein schauriges
Thema. Literarische Parodien." Neue deutsche Literatur,
13, No. 4(1965), 141-45.
567 Tank, Kurt Lothar. Günter Grass. Berlin: Colloquium,
1965; 5th. rev. and enlarged edn. 1974.
568 "Verleihung des Georg-Büchner-Preises an Günter Grass. Be-
grüssungsansprache von Ernst Schütte; Rede auf den Preisträger von Kasimir Edschmid; Rede über das Selbstverständliche von Günter Grass." Jahrbuch der Deutschen Akademie
für Sprache und Dichtung (1965), pp. 78-108.
569 Verleihung des Georg-Büchner-Preises 1965 an Günter Grass.
Festrede von Ernst Schütte. Laudatio von Kasimir Edschmid. Neuwied: Luchterhand, 1965, 15 pp.
570 Zatons'kyj, Dmytro Volodymyrovyč. "Antyheroj." Heroj i
antyheroj (Kiev: Izd-vo "Naukova dumka," 1965), pp. 145-
75.
571 Zimmermann, Werner. "Von Ernst Wiechert zu Günter Grass.
Probleme der Auswahl zeitgenössischer Literatur im
Deutschunterricht des Gymnasiums." Wirkendes Wort, 15
(1965), 316-26.

1966

572 Brügge, Peter. "Erst NPD wählen, dann nach dem Programm
fragen." Der Spiegel, 20 (21 November 1966), 177.
573 Cunliffe, W.G. "Aspects of the Absurd in Günter Grass."
Wisconsin Studies in Contemporary Literature, 7, No. 3
(Autumn 1966), 311-27.
574 Dünnebier, Anna. "Dichter, Helden & Grass." Radio
Bremen, Hausbuch 1966, pp. 161-65.
575 Fischer, Heinz. "Exorcismo de la lengua alemana. Obser-
vaciones sobre la obra de Heinrich Böll y Günter Grass."
Filología Moderna (Madrid), 6, No. 21/22(1966), 29-42.
576 Fried, Erich. "Princeton-Nachlese. -- Grass-Grässlich-
keiten oder Man kann den Grass wachsen hören." Kürbiskern, No. 4(1966), p. 98.
577 Holthusen, Hans Egon. "Günter Grass als politischer
Autor." Der Monat, 18, No. 216 (1966), 66-81.
578 Jensen, Jørgen Bonde. "Kunstner og engagement." Vind-
rosen (Copenhagen), 13, No. 5(1966), 44-58.
579 Karfíkova, Věra. "Günter Grass v Praze." Literárni
Noviny, 15, No. 44(1966), 9.
580 Mayer-Amery, Christian. "Gruppe 47 at Princeton."
Nation, 202(16 May 1966), 588-90.
581 Mlechina, T. "Grass's Wrong Turn." Trans. anon. from
Russian. Atlas, 12(December 1966), 48-50.

582 Mletschina, Irina. "Tertium non datur." Trans. from
     Russian by Rita Braun. Sinn und Form, 18(1966), 1258-62;
     Die Presse der Sowjetunion (Berlin), 96(1966); Sonntag
     (Berlin), 34(1966).
583 Neveux, J.B. "Günter Grass le Vistulien." Etudes Ger-
     maniques, 21(1966), 527-50.
584 Pike, Burton. "Objects vs. People in the recent German
     novel." Contemporary Literature, 7(1966), 301-10.
585 Pongs, Hermann. Dichtung im gespaltenen Deutschland.
     Stuttgart: Union Verlag, 1966, pp. 36-40 (Katz und Maus),
     423-26 (Die Blechtrommel), 481-82 (Die Plebejer proben den
     Aufstand).
586 Salyámosy, Miklós. "Günter Grass." A német irodalom a
     XX. században. Szerkesztette és a bevezetöt irta Vajda
     György Mihály (Budapest: Gondolat, 1966), pp. 493-507.
587 Subiotto, Arrigo. "Günter Grass." Essays on contemporary
     German Literature. German Men of Letters, Vol IV, ed.
     Brian Keith-Smith (London: Wolff, 1966), pp. 215-35.
588 -yt "Das böse Beispiel Günter Grass." Deutsche Studien,
     4(1966), 489-90.

     1967

589 Anon. "Grass wirbt für die FDP." Abendzeitung (München),
     28 February 1967, p. 1.
590 Anon. "Grass: Wiedervereinigung." Abendzeitung (Mün-
     chen), 28 February 1967, p. 5.
591 Anon. "Not des Bürgers." Der Spiegel, 21(2 October
     1967), 186-88.
592 Anon. "Grass contra Springer." Die Zeit, 3 October 1967,
     pp. 9-10.
593 Bondy, François. "Avec Günter Grass." Preuves, No. 194
     (April 1967), pp. 30-34.
594 Chotjewitz, Peter O. "Millionen Bild-Leser fordern: Gebt
     Günter Grass einen offiziellen Empfang," Streit-Zeit-
     Schrift, 6, No. 1 (1967), 48-52.
595 Fischer, Heinz. "Sprachliche Tendenzen bei Heinrich Böll
     und Günter Grass." German Quarterly, 40(1967), 372-83.
596 Hacks, Peter. "Schnauzbärtige Kleinbürger! Peter Hacks
     über seinen Plan einer 'deutschen Komödie!'" Der Spiegel,
     21(23 January 1967), 91.
597 Holthusen, Hans Egon. "Günter Grass als politischer
     Autor." Plädoyer für den Einzelnen (München: Piper,
     1967), pp. 40-68.
598 Honsza, Norbert. "Günter Grass." Kultura (Warsaw), 5,
     No. 30(1967), 3-5 (in Polish).
599 Lettau, Reinhard (ed.). Die Gruppe 47: Bericht, Kritik,
     Polemik. Neuwied: Luchterhand, 1967, passim.
600 Mayer, Hans. Zur deutschen Literatur der Zeit: Zusammen-
     hänge, Schriftsteller, Bücher. Reinbek: Rowohlt, 1967,
     passim.

601 Nechuschtan, Abner. "Bekenntnis und Kritik: Günter Grass
     in Israel." Europäische Begegnung (Braunschweig), 7
     (1967), 269-70.
602 Stuckenschmidt, H.H. "Musik zu Lindegren, Grass, Pavese
     in Berliner Konzertsälen." Melos, 34(1967), 175-77.
603 Václavek, Ludvík. "Literaturen der kulturellen Vermitt-
     lung." Philologica Pragensia (Prague), 10(1967), 193-202
     (Grass: 198-99).
604 Yates, Norris W. Günter Grass. A Critical Essay. Grand
     Rapids, Michigan: William B. Eerdmans, 1967, 48 pp.
605 Zimmer, Dieter. "Politik interessiert zur Zeit mehr."
     Die Zeit, 24 October 1967, p. 17.

1968

606 Büscher, Heiko. "Günter Grass." Deutsche Literatur seit
     1945 in Einzeldarstellungen, ed. Dietrich Weber (Stutt-
     gart: Kröner, 1968), pp. 455-83; 2nd. rev. ed. 1971, pp.
     506-34.
607 Forster, Leonard. "Günter Grass." University of Toronto
     Quarterly, 38, No. 1 (October 1968), 1-16.
608 Hamm, Peter. "Grass und seine Kritiker." Der Spiegel,
     22(2 December 1968), 190-93.
609 Horst, Karl August. "Über Günter Grass." Neue Zürcher
     Zeitung, 27 October 1968, pp. 49-50.
610 Ide, Heinz. "Dialektisches Denken im Werk von Günter
     Grass." Studium Generale, 21(1968), 608-22.
611 Knudsen, Jørgen. "Günter Grass." Fremmede digtere i det
     20. århundrede. Vol. 3, ed. Sven M. Kristensen (Copen-
     hagen: G.E.C. Grad, 1968), pp. 551-68.
612 Mann, Golo. "Hiergeblieben. Der Staat sind wir." Frank-
     furter Allgemeine Zeitung, 18 May 1968, p. 20.
613 Wegener, Adolph. "Günter Grass, der realistische Zauber-
     lehrling." Helen Adolf Festschrift, ed. Sheema Z. Buehne,
     James L. Hodge, and Lucille B. Pinto (New York: Ungar,
     1968), pp. 285-98.
614 Wijkmark, Carl-Henning. "Günter Grass." Vandringer Med
     Böcker (Lund), 17, No. 8(1968), 1-4.

1969

615 Anon. "Sowas durchmachen." Der Spiegel, 23(11 August
     1969), 86-100.
616 Anon. "Günter Grass." Stern, 22, No. 41(12 October
     1969), 9.
617 Anon. Kunst oder Pornographie? Der Prozess Grass gegen
     Ziesel. Eine Dokumentation. München: Lehmann, 1969.
     88 pp.
618 Cunliffe, W. Gordon. Günter Grass. Twayne's World
     Authors Series 65. New York: Twayne, 1969.

35

619 Dobozy, I. "Der Irrtum des Günter Grass." Neues Deutschland, No. 46 (1969).
620 Esser, Josef. "Grass täuscht sich in SPD und Demokratie."
Die Zeit, 25 February 1969, p. 20.
621 Grunenberg, Nina. "Günter Grass an der SPD-Front." Die
Zeit, 1 April 1969, p. 9.
622 Hassner, Pierre. "Wie viele Deutschlands." Die Zeit, 4
February 1969, p. 9.
623 Hoffman, Gerhard H. "Günter Grass und Ostdeutschland."
Politische Studien, 20, No. 183(1969), 53-59.
624 Isbăşescu, Mihai. "Günter Grass şi forţa epicului."
Secolul 20 (Bucharest), 9, No. 5(1969), 65-70.
625 Kaiser, Joachim. "Wie einst die Gruppe 47." Die Zeit,
20 May 1969, p. 13.
626 Krüger, Horst. "Des Kanzlers Klage." Die Zeit, 25 March
1969, p. 11.
627 Krüger, Horst. "Das Wappentier der Republik." Die Zeit
(U.S. Edition), 29 April 1969, p. 11.
628 Krüger, Horst. "Das Wappentier der Republik." Deutsche
Augenblicke (München: Piper, 1969), pp. 128-34.
629 Kurz, Paul K., S.J. "Von und über Günter Grass: Über
neue literarische Erscheinungen." Stimmen der Zeit, 183
(1969), 321-29.
630 Kurz, Paul Konrad. "Kunst oder Pornographie?" Stimmen
der Zeit, 184(1969), 136-38.
631 Leonard, Irène. "Engagement und Günter Grass." Beiträge
zu den Sommerkursen (München: Goethe-Institut, 1969), pp.
66-78.
632 Leonhardt, Rudolf Walter. "Die Sorgen des PEN." Die
Zeit, 6 May 1969, p. 13.
633 Raymont, Henry. "Frankfurt: Buffoons and Tragedians."
American-German Review, 35, No. 2(1969), 13-17.
634 Recktenwald, Wilhelm H. "Günter Grass. 'Enfant terrible'
der deutschen Gegenwartsliteratur." Beiträge zu den
Sommerkursen (München: Goethe-Institut, 1969), pp. 57-65.
635 Schwarz, Wilhelm Johannes. Der Erzähler Günter Grass.
Bern, München: Francke, 1969; 2nd. edn. 1971.
636 Scott, Nathan A., Jr. Negative capability: studies in the
new literature and the religious situation. New Haven,
London: Yale University Press, 1969.
637 Tank, Kurt Lothar. Günter Grass. Trans. John Conway.
Modern Literature Monographs. New York: Frederick Ungar,
1969.
638 Ude, Karl. "Günter Grass und das Christentum." Welt und
Wort, 24(1969), 180.
639 Uhlig, Gudrun. "Günter Grass." Autor, Werk und Kritik:
Inhaltsangaben, Kritiken und Textproben für den Literatur-
unterricht. Bd. 1 (München: Hueber, 1969), pp. 68-94.
640 Zimmer, Dieter. "Ein Verlag der Autoren." Die Zeit, 4
March 1969, p. 9.

641 Zundel, Rolf. "Mit der Macht auf du und du." Die Zeit,
     29 April 1969, p. 4.
642 Zundel, Rolf. "Die SPD ist verstört." Die Zeit, 20 May
     1969, p. 4.

1970

643 Ascherson, Neal. "The lonely German." The Observer
     (London), 26 July 1970, p. 7.
644 Bürke, Georg. "Günter Grass sucht seinen Ort." Orien-
     tierung (Zürich), 34, No. 6/7 (1970), 72-74; and 34, No.
     8 (1970), 83-85.
645 Dahne, G. "Zur Problematik des Geschichtsbewusstseins im
     Werk von Günter Grass." Diss. Greifswald, 1970.
646 Hobson, Harold. "Rebel in trouble." Sunday Times, 26
     July 1970.
647 Honsza, Norbert. "Lewica z poprawką." Poglady (Kato-
     wice), 8, No. 23 (1970), 17-18.
648 Jappe, Georg. "Zwischen allen Stühlen." Die Zeit, 15
     December 1970, p. 9.
649 Karasek, Hellmuth. Deutschland deine Dichter: Die Feder-
     halter der Nation (Hamburg: Hoffmann & Campe, 1970), pp.
     72-74, 80-85, and passim.
650 Krüger, Horst. "Ohne Macht und Mandat." Die Zeit, 7 July
     1970, p. 8.
651 Pavlova, N. "Gjunter Grass i studenty." Teatr (Moscow),
     31, No. 6 (1970), 132-33.
652 Reich-Ranicki, Marcel. "Einhundertvierzig deutsche Dich-
     ter." Die Zeit, 24 March 1970, p. 9.
653 von Vegesack, Thomas. Inte bara Grass . . . De tyska
     litteraturerna efter kriget. Stockholm: Norstedts förlag,
     1970.
654 Werth, Wolfgang. "Vergangenheit zieht aus." Merian, 23,
     No. 1 (1970), 82-84.
655 Willson, A. Leslie. "Perspective: The Dance of Art."
     Dimension, Special Issue 1970, pp. 7-21; rpt. Willson,
     A Günter Grass Symposium (1971), pp. 3-17.

1971

656 Arnold, Heinz Ludwig and Franz Josef Görtz (eds.). Günter
     Grass--Dokumente zur politischen Wirkung. Edition Text +
     Kritik. Stuttgart: Richard Boorberg, 1971.
657 Ahlsson, Lars-Eric. "Zur Wortbildung bei Günter Grass.
     Das zusammengesetzte Adjektiv." Studia neophilologica
     (Stockholm), 43 (1971), 180-97.
658 Ascherson, Neal. "The man who bangs the drum for modera-
     tion." Observer, colour supplement, 18 April 1971, p. 10.
659 Bosch, Manfred. "Der Literaturgarten." Das Pult, 3, No.
     1 (1971), 11-12.
660 Di Napoli, Thomas John. "The rhetoric of religion in the

works of Günter Grass." Diss. University of Texas at
Austin, 1971. <u>Dissertation Abstracts International</u>, 33
(1972/73), 305A.

661 Durzak, Manfred. <u>Arno Holz, Alfred Döblin, Günter Grass:
Zur Tradition von politischer Dichtung in Deutschland.</u>
Language Monographs 13. Saltsjö-Duvnäs: Moderna Spräk,
1971. 21pp.

662 Everett, George Alexander. "Perceptive intent in the
works of Günter Grass. An investigation and assessment
with extensive bibliography." Diss. Louisiana State University, 1971. <u>Dissertation Abstracts</u>, 32(1971/72),
2683A.

663 Fisson, Pierre. "L'irresistible ascension de Gunter
Grass." <u>Figaro litteraire</u>, No. 1289 (February 1971), pp.
16-17.

664 Herburger, Günter. "Überlebensgross Herr Grass." <u>Die
Zeit</u>, 4 June 1971, p. 13.

665 Jäger, Manfred. "Der politische Günter Grass." <u>Text +
Kritik</u>, No. 1/1a, 4. Aufl. (1971), pp. 74-84.

666 Jaesrich, Hellmut. "Günter Grass, or Dragon Hunting."
<u>Encounter</u> (London), 37(November 1971), 60-64.

667 Kaiser, J. "Günter Grass oder Das erfüllte Image." <u>Füh-
rer und Verführer: Geist und Mode unserer Zeit</u>, ed. L.
Reiwisch and K. Hoffmann (München: Droemer-Knaur, 1971),
pp. 193-205.

668 Krüger, Horst. "Ritratto di Günter Grass." <u>Settanta</u>,
14-15 (1971), 61-62.

669 Labhardt, Robert and Rudolf Walther. "Günter Grass. Bericht und Werkanalyse." <u>Der Schriftsteller und sein Verhältnis zur Sprache, dargestellt am Problem der Tempus-
wahl</u>, ed. Peter André Bloch (Bern: Francke, 1971), pp.
289-90.

670 Mason, Ann Lois. "Günter Grass' Conception of the Artist." Diss. Cornell University 1971. <u>Dissertation Abstracts International</u>, 32 (1971), 443A.

671 Anon. <u>Moderne Deutsche Schriftsteller. Kurzdokumentation
No. 3: Günter Grass.</u> Zusammengestellt von Inter Nationes,
Referat Information. Bonn: Inter Nationes, 1971. 28pp.

672 Pross, Harry. "Kritik als Fürsprache: Günter Grass."
<u>Söhne der Kassandra. Versuch über deutsche Intellektuelle</u>
(Stuttgart: Kohlhammer, 1971), pp. 131-41.

673 Willson, A. Leslie. <u>A Günter Grass Symposium.</u> Published
for the Department of Germanic Languages. The University
of Texas at Austin. Austin and London: University of
Texas Press, 1971.

1972

674 Barthe, Raymond. "A Paris, Günter Grass parle de la
'Melencholia' de Dürer." <u>La Quinzaine Littéraire</u> (Paris),
No. 133(1972), pp. 9-10.

675 Deschner, Karlheinz. "Runter mit der Glorie von Günter Grass. Kleine Lehrstunde über die grossen Schludrigkeiten eines bekannten Autors." Pardon, No. 11 (1972), pp. 42-44.

676 Frisch, Max. "Album." Tagebuch 1966-1971 (Frankfurt: Suhrkamp, 1972), pp. 325-35.

677 Lebeau, Jean. "Individu et société: ou la métamorphose de Günter Grass." Recherches Germaniques (Strasbourg), No. 2 (1972), pp. 68-93.

678 Leonard, Irène. "Banging the drum." New Society, 22 (9 November 1972), 321.

679 Nelson, M. "The grotesque and the ludicrous in Günter Bruno Fuchs, Günter Grass, Kurt Kusenberg, and Wolfdietrich Schnurre" (Synopsis). AULLA: Proceedings and papers, 14(1972), 180.

680 Šliažas, Rimvydas. "Günter Grass." Metmenys (Chicago), 23(1972), 77-92.

1973

681 Anon. "Anstoss gegeben." Der Spiegel, 27(10 September 1973), 23-24.

682 Gerhardt, Marlis. "Günter Grass.--Texte von Günter Grass." Der Friede und die Unruhestifter, ed. Hans Jürgen Schultz (Frankfurt: Suhrkamp, 1973), pp. 305-22.

683 Jurgensen, Manfred (ed.). Grass: Kritik--Thesen--Analysen. Queensland Studies in German Language and Literature, 4. Bern, München: Francke, 1973.

684 Leonard, Irène. "The problem of commitment in the work of Günter Grass." M. Phil. Thesis. University of London, 1973.

685 Mason, Ann L. "Beyond storytelling: New directions in Grass criticism." Diacritics, 3, No. 2(1973), 10-14.

686 Mieder, Wolfgang. "Günter Grass und das Sprichwort." Muttersprache, 83, No. 1(1973), 64-67.

687 Schwarz, Wilhelm J. "Günter Grass." Deutsche Dichter der Gegenwart, ed. Benno von Wiese (Berlin: Erich Schmidt, 1973), pp. 560-72.

688 Tank, Kurt Lothar. "Deutsche Politik im literarischen Werk von Günter Grass." Grass: Kritik--Thesen--Analysen, ed. Manfred Jurgensen (Bern: Francke, 1973), pp. 167-89.

1974

689 Enderstein, Carl O. "Zahnsymbolik und ihre Bedeutung in Günter Grass' Werken." Monatshefte, 66(1974), 5-18.

690 Hayman, Ronald. "Günter Grass." Playback (New York: Horizon Press, 1974), pp. 167-77.

691 Jurgensen, Manfred. Über Günter Grass: Untersuchungen zur sprachbildlichen Rollenfunktion. Bern, München: Francke, 1974.

692 Leonard, Irène. Günter Grass. Edinburgh: Oliver & Boyd, 1974.

693 Mason, Ann L. The skeptical muse: A study of Günter Grass' conception of the artist. Bern, Frankfurt: Herbert Lang, 1974.

694 Reich-Ranicki, Marcel. "Erfolg und Ruhm." Frankfurter Allgemeine Zeitung, 23 October 1974, p. 25.

695 Schreiber, Mathias. "Grass contra Sinjawski." Deutsche Zeitung, 18 October 1974, p. 9.

696 Thomas, R. Hinton, and K. Bullivant. Literature in Upheaval: West German Writers and the Challenge of the 1960's. Manchester: Manchester University Press, 1974, passim.

1975

697 Cepl-Kaufmann, Gertrude. Günter Grass: Eine Analyse des Gesamtwerkes unter dem Aspekt von Literatur und Politik. Kronberg/Ts.: Scriptor Verlag, 1975.

698 Monteil, Annemarie. "Ein Aufklärer ohne Dogmatismus." Basler Nationalzeitung, 12 March 1975.

III. F I C T I O N

0 / The Fiction in general

1962

699 Ziesel, Kurt. Die Literaturfabrik. Eine polemische Auseinandersetzung mit dem Literaturbetrieb im Deutschland von heute. Wien/Köln, 1962.

1963

700 Hyman, Stanley Edgar. "An inept symbolist." New Leader, 46(19 August 1963), 16-17.

701 Reich-Ranicki, Marcel. "Günter Grass, unser grimmiger Idylliker." Deutsche Literatur in West und Ost. Prosa seit 1945 (München: Piper, 1963), pp. 216-30; Hamburg: Rowohlt, 1970, pp. 148-58.

1964

702 Anon. "Novels of 1963: Günter Grass: Hundejahre, Cat and Mouse." T/L/S: Essays and Reviews from the Times Literary Supplement, 1963, Vol. II (London: Oxford University Press, 1964), pp. 67-71.

703 Baumgart, Reinhard. "Kleinbürgertum und Realismus. Über-

legungen zu Romanen von Böll, Grass und Johnson." Neue Rundschau, 75(1964), 650-64.

704 Heiseler, Bernt von. "Günter Grass, Die Blechtrommel, Katz und Maus, Hundejahre." Der Kranich, 6(1964), 151-52.

705 Jerde, C.D. "A Corridor of Pathos: Notes on the Fiction of Günter Grass." The Minnesota Review, 4, No. 4(Summer 1964), 558-60.

706 Oppen, Beate Ruhm von. "Two German Writers of the Sixties." Massachusetts Review, 5(Summer 1964), 769-78.

707 Plotnick, Harvey. "Speculations about Germany." Modern Age, 8(Summer 1964), 330-32.

1965

708 Hamburger, Michael. From Prophecy to Exorcism: The premisses of modern German Literature (London: Longmans, 1965), pp. 150-58.

709 Höllerer, Walter. "Die Bedeutung des Augenblicks im modernen Romananfang." Romananfänge--Versuch zu einer Poetik des Romans, ed. Norbert Miller (Berlin, Literarisches Colloquium, 1965), pp. 344-77.

710 Neubert, Werner. "Die Groteske in unserer Zeit." Neue deutsche Literatur, 13, No. 1(1965), 102-16.

1966

711 Enright, D.J. "Three New Germans. Günter Grass." Conspirators and Poets (London: Chatto & Windus, 1966), pp. 190-193.

712 Hyman, Stanley Edgar. "An Inept Symbolist: Günter Grass." Standards: A Chronicle of Books for Our Time (New York: Horizon, 1966), pp. 168-72.

1967

713 Dornheim, Alfredo. "Ernst Kreuder y Günter Grass. La realidad interior en la narrativa contemporanea de Alemania." Boletín de estudios germanicos, 6(1967), 125-34; German translation: "Ernst Kreuder und Günter Grass: innere Wirklichkeit in der gegenwärtigen deutschen Prosa," pp. 135-45.

714 Hatfield, Henry. "Günter Grass: The Artist as Satirist." The Contemporary Novel in German: A Symposium, ed. Robert R. Heitner (Austin: University of Texas Press, 1967), pp. 115-34.

715 Moore, Harry T. "Three Group 47 novelists: Böll, Johnson, Grass." Twentieth-Century German Literature (New York, London: Basic Books, 1967), pp. 192-206, esp. 200-206.

716 Parry, Idris. "Aspects of Günter Grass's Narrative Technique." Forum for Modern Language Studies, 3(1967), 99-114.

41

717 Ritter, Jesse P., Jr. "Fearful Comedy: The Fiction of
     Joseph Heller, Günter Grass, and the Social Surrealist
     Genre." Diss. Arkansas, 1967. Dissertation Abstracts,
     28(1967), 1447A.
718 Welzig, Werner. Der deutsche Roman im 20. Jahrhundert.
     Stuttgart: Kröner, 1967, pp. 262-67 and passim.

     1968

719 Cwojdrak, G. "Das epische Panoptikum des Günter Grass."
     Eine Prise Polemik (Halle: Mitteldeutscher Verl, 1968),
     pp. 101-14.
720 Mandel, Siegfried. "The German Novel: In the Wake of
     Organized Madness." Contemporary European Novelists, ed.
     Siegfried Mandel (Carbondale: Southern Illinois University
     Press, 1968), pp. 69-125, esp. 109-124.
721 Piirainen, Ilpo Tapani. Textbezogene Untersuchungen über
     "Katz und Maus" und "Hundejahre" von Günter Grass. Euro-
     päische Hochschulschriften, I, 11. Bern: Lang, 1968.
722 Thomas, R. Hinton, and Wilfried van der Will. "Günter
     Grass." The German Novel and the Affluent Society (Man-
     chester: Manchester University Press, 1968), pp. 68-85.

     1969

723 Baker, Ronald Alfred. "Animal Imagery in the Novels of
     Günter Grass." Diss. Harvard 1969.
724 Hatfield, Henry. "The Arist as Satirist: Günter Grass."
     Crisis and Continuity in Modern German Fiction: Ten Essays
     (Ithaca, N.Y., and London: Cornell University Press,
     1969), pp. 128-49.
725 Reddick, John. "The eccentric narrative world of Günter
     Grass: aspects of Die Blechtrommel, Katz und Maus and
     Hundejahre." D. Phil. diss. University of Oxford, 1969.
726 Sodeikat, Ernst. "Schrieb Günter Grass eine Danzig-Saga?
     Ergebnisse einer Analyse der Bücher Die Blechtrommel und
     Hundejahre." "Als Manuskript gedruckt Hannover 1969."
     16pp.
727 Thomas, R. Hinton, and Wilfried van der Will. "Günter
     Grass." Der deutsche Roman und die Wohlstandsgesellschaft
     (Stuttgart: Kohlhammer, 1969), pp. 80-102.

     1970

728 Demetz, Peter. "Günter Grass." Postwar German Litera-
     ture: A critical introduction (New York: Pegasus, 1970),
     pp. 214-29; rpt. New York: Schocken Books, 1972.
729 Eykman, Christoph. "Absurde Mechanik. Die 'verunglimpfte'
     Geschichte in den Romanen von Günter Grass." Geschichts-
     pessimismus in der deutschen Literatur des zwanzigsten
     Jahrhunderts (Bern: Francke, 1970), pp. 112-24.

730 Freedman, Ralph. "The Poet's Dilemma: The Narrative Worlds of Günter Grass." Dimension, Special Issue 1970, pp. 50-63; rpt. A. Leslie Willson, A Günter Grass Symposium (1971), pp. 46-59.

731 Hartung, Günter. "Bobrowski und Grass." Weimarer Beiträge, 16, No. 8(1970), 203-24.

732 Horsley, Ritta Jo. "Recollection in the fiction of Günter Grass: Technique and Theme." Diss. Harvard 1970.

733 Rosenthal, Erwin Theodor. "Erzählhaltung und Perspektivenwechsel: Fichte, Beckett, Grass." Das Fragmentarische Universum (München: Nymphenburg, 1970), pp. 139-52.

734 Zimmer, Hildegard G. "A comparison of the last three novels of Thomas Mann and the first three of Günter Grass." M.A. Thesis, University of Toronto, 1970.

1971

735 Böschenstein, Bernhard. "Günter Grass als Nachfolger Jean Pauls und Döblins." Jahrbuch der Jean-Paul-Gesellschaft, 6(1971), 86-101.

736 Eykman, Christoph. "Der Verlust der Geschichte in der deutschen Literatur des zwanzigsten Jahrhunderts." Neophilologus, 55, No. 1(1971), 58-72.

737 Forster, Leonard. "El arte narrativo de Günter Grass." Cuadernos de filología, December 1971, pp. 5-24.

738 Ghurye, Charlotte W. The Movement toward a New Social and Political Consciousness in Postwar German Prose. Bern: Lang, 1971, pp. 33-42 (Die Blechtrommel, Hundejahre); pp. 67-73 (Hundejahre).

739 Moore, David Pittman. "Günter Grass and Alejandro Nuñez Alonso. A comparative study of their novels." Diss. University of Arkansas, 1971. Dissertation Abstracts International, 32(1971/72), 977A.

740 Reddick, John. "Eine epische Trilogie des Leidens? Die Blechtrommel, Katz und Maus, Hundejahre." Text + Kritik, No. 1/1a, 4. Aufl. (1971), pp. 38-51.

741 van Vreckem, Paul. "Günter Grass' trilogie als kaleidoscoop." Nieuw Vlaams Tijdschrift, 24(1971), 169-91.

742 Yates, Norris W. "Günter Grass (1927-   )." The Politics of Twentieth-century Novelists, ed. George A. Panichas (New York: Hawthorn Books, 1971), pp. 215-28.

743 Yuill, W.E. "Tradition and Nightmare: Some Reflections on the Postwar Novel in England and Germany." Affinities: Essays in German and English Literature, ed. Rex W. Last (London: Oswald Wolff, 1971).

1972

744 Balotă, Nicolae. "Examen de conştiinţă in proza germana contemporană." Steaua, 23, No. 20(1972), 24-25.

745   Forster, Leonard. "Günter Grass, romancista." Colóquio, 7(1972), 12-20.

746   Parry, Idris. "The tree of movement." Animals of silence: Essays on art, nature, and folk-tale (London: Oxford U.P., 1972), pp. 19-26.

1973

747   Beyersdorf, Herman. "Childhood and adolescence in the prose works of Günter Grass" (Synopsis). Australasian Universities Language and Literature Association: Proceedings and papers, 15(1973), 11 and 14.

748   Demetz, Peter. "Günter Grass." Die süsse Anarchie (Frankfurt: Propyläen Verlag, 1973), pp. 254-72.

749   Kellermann, Rolf. "Günter Grass und Alfred Döblin." Grass: Kritik--Thesen--Analysen, ed. Manfred Jurgensen (Bern: Francke, 1973), pp. 107-50.

750   Lewis, Norman Howard. "An analysis of the theme of guilt and responsibility in selected works of Günter Grass." Diss. University of Iowa, 1973. Dissertation Abstracts International, 35(1974), 462A.

751   Ter-Nedden, Gisbert. "Allegorie und Geschichte. Zeit- und Sozialkritik als Formproblem des deutschen Romans der Gegenwart." Poesie und Politik: Zur Situation der Literatur in Deutschland, ed. Wolfgang Kuttenkeuler (Stuttgart: Kohlhammer, 1973), pp. 155-83.

1974

752   Ezergailis, Inta M. "Günter Grass's 'Fearful Symmetry': Dialectic, Mock and Real, in Katz und Maus and Die Blechtrommel." Texas Studies in Literature and Language, 16 (1974), 221-35.

753   Reddick, John. "Vom Pferdekopf zur Schnecke: Die Prosawerke von Günter Grass zwischen Beinahe-Verzweiflung und zweifelnder Hoffnung." Positionen im deutschen Roman der sechziger Jahre, ed. Heinz Ludwig Arnold and Theo Buck (Munich: Boorberg, 1974), pp. 39-54.

1975

754   Baker, Donna. "Nazism and the petit bourgeois protagonist: The novels of Grass, Böll and Mann." new german critique, No. 5(Spring 1975), pp. 77-106.

755   Reddick, John. The "Danzig Trilogy" of Günter Grass. London: Secker & Warburg, 1975.

756   Sann, Gisela. "Funktion der Frauenfiguren im Prosawerk von Günter Grass." Diss. McGill University, Montreal, 1975.

1958

757 Kaiser, Joachim. "Die Gruppe 47 lebt auf" (Meeting at Grossholzleute). Süddeutsche Zeitung (München), 5 November 1958.

1959

758 Anon. "Der Trommelbube." Der Spiegel, 13(18 November 1959), 80-82.
759 Arnold, Fritz. "Aus der Zwergperspektive." Augsburger Allgemeine, 5/6 December 1959.
760 Blöcker, Günter. "Rückkehr zur Nabelschnur." Frankfurter Allgemeine Zeitung, 28 November 1959; rpt. Loschütz, Von Buch zu Buch (1963), pp. 21-24.
761 Braem, Helmut M. "Narr mit dem Janusgesicht." Stuttgarter Zeitung, 24 October 1959, p. 52.
762 Eimers, Enno W. "Ein Schelmenroman unserer Tage--voll innerer Gesichte." Der Kurier (Berlin), 28 November 1959.
763 Enzensberger, Hans Magnus. "Wilhelm Meister, auf Blech getrommelt." Frankfurter Hefte, 14(November 1959), 833-36; Süddeutscher Rundfunk (Stuttgart), 18 November 1959; rpt. Einzelheiten (Frankfurt: Suhrkamp, 1962), pp. 221-27; rpt. Loschütz, Von Buch zu Buch (1968), pp. 8-12.
764 Fink, Humbert. "Ein Zwerg haut auf die Trommel." Heute (Wien), 12 December 1959.
765 Hamm, Peter. "Verrückte Lehr- und Wanderjahre." Du, 19, No. 12(1959), 132-36.
766 Hartlaub, Geno. "Eros und Sexus in der modernen Literatur." Sonntagsblatt (Hamburg), 15 November 1959.
767 Höllerer, Walter. "Roman im Kreuzfeuer." Tagesspiegel (Berlin), 20 December 1959; rpt. Loschütz, Von Buch zu Buch (1968), pp. 15-17.
768 Hornung, Peter. "Oskar Matzerath--Trommler und Gotteslästerer." Deutsche Tagespost (Würzburg), 23/24 November 1959; rpt. Loschütz, Von Buch zu Buch (1968), pp. 24-25.
769 Horst, Karl August. "Heimsuche." Merkur (Stuttgart), 13 (1959), 1191-95.
770 K., A. "Sprachmächtige Flucht aus der Verantwortung." Neues Winterthurer Tageblatt, 5 December 1959.
771 Kaiser, Joachim. "Oskars getrommelte Bekenntnisse." Süddeutsche Zeitung (München), 31 October 1959; rpt. Loschütz, Von Buch zu Buch (1968), pp. 13-15.
772 Kraus, Wolfgang. "Zwiespältiger Eindruck eines überdurchschnittlichen Romans." National-Zeitung (Basel), 19 December 1959.
773 Krolow, Karl. "Ist es nur ein Schelmenroman?" Neckar-Echo (Heilbronn), 21/22 November 1959.

774 Müller-Eckhard, H. "Die Blechtrommel." Kölnische Rundschau, 13 December 1959, p. 23.
775 Nolte, Jost. "Oskar, der Trommler, kennt keine Tabu." Die Welt, 17 October 1959.
776 Schonauer, Franz. "Kindertrommel und schwarze Köchin." Stuttgarter Nachrichten, 17 October 1959, p. 34.
777 Tank, Kurt Lothar. "Der Blechtrommler schrieb Memoiren." Die Welt, 4 October 1959.
778 Uhlig, Herbert. "Die Trommel ist sein Tick." Der Tag (Berlin), 13 September 1959.
779 Widmer, Walter. "Geniale Verruchtheit." Basler Nachrichten, 18 December 1959; rpt. Loschütz, Von Buch zu Buch (1968), pp. 18-21.
780 Wien, Werner. "Trauermarsch auf der Blechtrommel." Christ und Welt (Stuttgart), 17 December 1959.
781 Wieser, Theodor. "Die Blechtrommel. Fabulierer und Moralist." Merkur, 13(1959), 1188-91.

1960

782 Bänziger, Hans. "Zwergengetrommel zwischen Ost und West." Die Tat (Zürich), 9 January 1960.
783 Baie, Bernhard. "Trommelei auf Blech." Recklinghäuser Zeitung, 6/7 February 1960.
784 Baumgart, Reinhard. "Der grosse Bänkelsang." Neue deutsche Hefte, 6(1959/60), pp. 861-63.
785 Bondy, François. "Le 'scandale' Günter Grass." Preuves, No. 115(September 1960), p. 23.
786 Busch, Günter. "Der Mensch im Stande der Deformation." Zeitwende, 31(1960), 130-31.
787 Busch, Günter. "Spektakel und Desillusionierung." Wort in der Zeit, 6, No. 2(1960), 58-59.
788 Deschner, Karlheinz. "Aus Deutschlands Vergangenheit--Abrechnung oder Rechtfertigung." Geist und Zeit (Düsseldorf/Darmstadt), No. 2(1960), pp. 141-49, esp. 145-47.
789 G., E. "Ein Zauberer trommelt ein Märchen." Arbeiterzeitung (Wien), 6 January 1960.
790 Grözinger, Wolfgang. "Der Roman der Gegenwart: Zeichen an der Wand." Hochland (München), 52(1959/60), 176.
791 Hartung, Rudolf. "Schläge auf die Blechtrommel." Neue deutsche Hefte, No. 67(1960), pp. 1053-56.
792 Herchenröder, Jan. "Ein Trommelfeuer von Einfällen." Die Andere Zeitung (Hamburg), March 1960.
793 Höllerer, Walter. "Letter from Germany." Evergreen Review, 4(November-December 1960), 135-38.
794 Humm/Loetscher. "Gepfiffen und getrommelt." Die Weltwoche (Zürich), 22 January 1960.
795 K. "Die Blechtrommel." Unser Danzig (Lübeck), 20 May 1960; rpt. Loschütz, Von Buch zu Buch (1968), pp. 25-26.
796 Kant, Hermann. "Ein Solo in Blech." Neue Deutsche Literatur (Berlin), 8, No. 5(1960), 151-55.

797 Leber, Hugo. "Der kaschubische Trommler." Tagesanzeiger für Stadt und Kanton Zürich, 26 September 1960.

798 Maier, Hansgeorg. "Powerteh der angestrengten Anstössigkeit." Frankfurter Rundschau, 27 February 1960.

799 Meidinger-Geise, J. "Der Trommler Oskar. Zu Günter Grass, Die Blechtrommel." Blätter der Gesellschaft für christliche Kultur e.V. (Düsseldorf), 3, No. 1/2(1960), 18-19.

800 Mieg, Peter. "Die Blechtrommel." Badener Tagblatt, 12 February 1960.

801 Migner, Karl. "Der getrommelte Protest gegen unsere Welt: Anmerkungen zu Günter Grass' Roman Die Blechtrommel." Welt und Wort, 15(1960), 205-207.

802 Reich-Ranicki, Marcel. "Auf gut Glück getrommelt." Die Zeit, 1 January 1960.

803 Röder, H. "Meisterliches, weniger Meisterliches." Tagebuch (Wien), 15, No. 12(1960).

804 Rp. "Hinter dem Guckloch, vor dem Guckloch." Deutsche Volkszeitung (Düsseldorf), 8 April 1960.

805 Valerius, E. "Giftzwerg Oskar rührt die blasphemische Blechtrommel." Das neue Journal (Wiesbaden), 8, No. 5 (1960), 33-35.

806 Wolffheim, Hans. "Trommelexcesse als Literatur." Hamburger Echo, 16 January 1960.

1961

807 Lewald, H.E. Books Abroad, 35(Autumn 1961), 339-40.

1962

808 Anon. "Drum of Neutrality." Times Literary Supplement, 5 October 1962, p. 776.

809 Ascherson, Neal. "Poison Dwarf." New Statesman, 64 (28 September 1962), 418.

810 Blöcker, Günter. "Günter Grass: Die Blechtrommel." Kritisches Lesebuch (Hamburg: Leibniz, 1962), pp. 208-15.

811 Carpelan, Bo. Hufstudstagsbladet (Helsinki), 28 December 1962.

812 Delez, Bernard. "Les lettres allemandes: un admirateur de Rabelais." La Revue Nouvelle, 35(1962), 285-87.

813 Faye, Jean-Pierre. "Le tambour de fer-blanc." Les Temps Modernes (Paris), 17(1962), 1176-80.

814 Garrett, Thomas J. "Oskars Empfang in England." Die Zeit, 26 October 1962.

815 Lerner, Laurence. Listener, 68(4 October 1962), 533.

816 Lodge, David. Spectator, 209(28 September 1962), 446.

817 Spender, Stephen. The Sunday Telegraph (London), 30 September 1962.

818 Woodtli, Susanna. "Die Blechtrommel." Reformatio (Zürich), 11(1962), 365-69.

47

819   Anon. "The guilt of the lambs." Time, 81(4 January 1963), 69-71.

820   Anon. "The Sound of Madness." Newsweek, 61(25 March 1963), 111.

821   Anon. Virginia Quarterly Review, 39(Spring 1963), xlix.

822   Barrett, William. Atlantic, 211(May 1963), 132, 134.

823   Bradbury, Malcolm. Punch, 244(23 January 1963), 140.

824   Burns, Richard K. Library Journal, 88(15 February 1963), 794.

825   Calisher, Hortense. Nation, 196(16 March 1963), 231-32.

826   Davenport, Guy. National Review, 14(9 April 1963), 287.

827   Emmel, Hildegard. Das Gericht in der deutschen Literatur des 20. Jahrhunderts (Bern und München: Francke, 1963), pp. 105-19.

828   Field, G.W. Queen's Quarterly, 70(1963), 461-62.

829   Gregory, Horace. "The ancient follies are still in the Ascendancy." Commonweal, 78(26 April 1963), 146-48.

830   Grumbach, Doris. Critic, 21(June 1963), 81.

831   Grunfeld, Fred. "Drums along the Vistula." Reporter, 28 (14 March 1963), 54-57.

832   Hanson, William P. "Oskar, Rasputin and Goethe." Canadian Modern Language Review, 20, No. 1(1963), 29-32.

833   Hochmann, Sandra. "The Tin Drum." The Village Voice (New York), 14 March 1963.

834   Horst, Karl A. "Wut ohne Pathos. Betrachtungen über einige neue Romane." Merkur (Köln), 17(1963), 1209-14.

835   Ihlenfeld, Kurt. "Oskar und sein Autor." Eckart-Jahrbuch, 1962/63, pp. 329-34.

836   Johnson, Lucy. "Loss of Innocence." Progressive, 27 (May 1963), 48-50.

837   Kozarynowa, Zofia. "Polonica u Günthera Grassa." Wiadomości (London), 21 July 1963, p. 2.

838   Lindley, Denver. "Disarming the Nazi era with gallows humor." New York Herald Tribune, 39(7 April 1963), 1 and 18.

839   McGovern, Hugh. America, 108(9 March 1963), 344.

840   Marcus, Steven. "A new beat." New York Review of Books, 1, No. 2(1963), 23.

841   Morton, Frederic. "Growing up with Oskar." New York Times Book Review, 68(7 April 1963), 5 and 58.

842   Pisco, Ernest S. "Satire from West Germany." Christian Science Monitor, 7 March 1963, p. 10.

843   Plant, Richard. "Rhythms of Pandemonium." Saturday Review, 46(9 March 1963), 35-36.

844   Plard, Henri. "Verteidigung der Blechtrommel. Über Günter Grass." Text + Kritik, No. 1(1963), pp. 1-8.

845   Quinn, John J. Best Seller, 23(1 April 1963), 12-13.

846   Rand, Max. Uusi Suomi (Helsinki), 5 May 1963.

847 Renek, Morris. "Ballyhoo." Midstream (New York), 9 (June 1963), 109-11.
848 Simon, John. "The Drummer of Danzig." Partisan Review, 30(Fall 1963), 446-53.
849 Vonalt, Larry P. "Barbaric, Mystical, Bored." Sewanee Review, 71(Summer 1963), 522-24.
850 West, Anthony. New Yorker, 39(27 April 1963), 169-70.
851 West, Paul. "Turning New Leaves." Canadian Forum, 43 (July 1963), 85-86.

1964

852 Andrews, R.C. "The Tin Drum." Modern Languages, 45, No. 1(1964), 28-31.
853 Holthusen, Hans Egon. Avantgardismus und die Zukunft der modernen Kunst. München: Piper, 1964, pp. 51-58.
854 Horst, Karl August. Das Abenteuer der deutschen Literatur im 20. Jahrhundert (München: Nymphenburg, 1964), passim.
855 Joppe, Jaap. Rotterdamsch Nieuwsblad, 21 November 1964.
856 Lörinc, Peter. Magyar Szó (Budapest), January 1964.
857 Tank, Kurt Lothar. ". . . mit Matzerath leben?" Sonntagsblatt (Hamburg), No. 22(1964), pp. 1-2.

1965

858 Friedrichsmeyer, Erhard M. "Aspects of myth, parody, and obscenity in Grass' Die Blechtrommel and Katz und Maus." The Germanic Review, 40(1965), 240-50.
859 Klöckner, Klaus. "Zuchtvoll entfesselt: Günter Grass. Die Blechtrommel." Pädagogische Provinz, 19(1965), 537-46.
860 Kuhn, Heinrich. "Tagwache auf der Blechtrommel gerührt." National-Zeitung (Basel), 18 July 1965.
861 Levitt, Morton Paul. "From a new point of view: Studies in the contemporary novel." Diss. Pennsylvania State University, 1965. Dissertation Abstracts, 26(1966), 6717.
862 Matsuda, Nobuo. "Die Komik in Grass' Roman Die Blechtrommel" (Japanese, German abstract). Doitsu Bungaku, 35 (1965), 1-11.
863 Suttner, Hans. "Blechtrommler auf Tournee." Echo der Zeit (Recklinghausen), 21 July 1965.

1966

864 Bier, Jean-Paul. "Les ambiguités de la périphrase: A propos du Tambour de Günter Grass." Socialisme (Brussels), No. 77(September 1966), pp. 690-95.
865 Blanch, Mable. "Variations on a picaresque theme: a study of two twentieth-century treatments of picaresque form." Diss. University of Colorado, 1966. Dissertation Ab-

stracts, 28(1967), 1427A.

866 Everett, George Alexander, Jr. "Swift's Gulliver's Travels and Grass' Die Blechtrommel." M.A. Thesis, Louisiana State University, Baton Rouge, Louisiana, 1966.

867 Fritzsching, Hubertus. "Günter Grass, Die Blechtrommel." Das Weltverständnis des deutschen Gegenwartsromans im Spiegel seiner Erzählhaltung (Würzburg, 1966), pp. 156-66.

868 Honsza, Norbert. "Günter Grass und kein Ende?" Annali Istituto Universitario Orientale, Napoli, Sezione Germanica, 9(1966), 177-87.

869 Ivey, Frederick M. The Tin Drum: or retreat to the Word. Wichita State University Studies, No. 66. Wichita, Ka.: Wichita State University, 1966.

870 Klinge, Reinhold. "Die Blechtrommel im Unterricht. Ein Versuch." Deutschunterricht, 18, No. 2(1966), 91-103.

871 Schumann, Willy. "Wiederkehr der Schelme." PMLA, 81 (1966), 467-74.

872 Sharfman, William L. "The Organization of Experience in The Tin Drum." The Minnesota Review, 6, No. 1(1966), 59-65.

873 Willson, A. Leslie. "The Grotesque Everyman in Günter Grass's Die Blechtrommel." Monatshefte, 58(1966), 131-38.

874 Woods, A. "A study of the novel Die Blechtrommel by Günter Grass." M.A. thesis Liverpool 1966.

1967

875 Bance, A.F. "The enigma of Oskar in Grass's Blechtrommel." Seminar, 3(1967), 147-56.

876 Buckeye, Robert. "The anatomy of the psychic novel." Critique (Minneapolis), 9, No. 2(1967), 33-45.

877 Damian, Hermann Siegfried. "Die Blechtrommel von Günter Grass: Versuch einer Analyse." M.A. Dissertation, University of Tasmania, 1967.

878 Ferguson, Lore Schefter. "Die Blechtrommel von Günter Grass: Versuch einer Interpretation." Diss., Ohio State University, 1967. Dissertation Abstracts, 28(1967), 1074A.

879 Gelley, Alexander. "Art and Reality in Die Blechtrommel." Forum for Modern Language Studies (University of St. Andrews, Scotland), 3(1967), 115-25.

880 Mayer, Hans. "Felix Krull und Oskar Matzerath: Aspekte des Romans." Süddeutsche Zeitung, 14/15 October 1967; rev. rpt. Das Geschehen und das Schweigen: Aspekte der Literatur (Frankfurt: Suhrkamp, 1969), pp. 35-67.

881 O'Nan, Martha. Günter Grass's Oskar. Occasional Papers in Language, Literature, and Linguistics (Ohio U.), A3. Athens: Ohio University, Modern Languages Dept., 1967 (pamphlet, mimeo, 9pp).

882 Smith, M.A. "The Tin Drum by Gunter Grass." Kolokon, 2 (Spring 1967), 48-52.

883 Van der Will, Wilfried. "Die Blechtrommel." Pikaro
     heute: Metamorphosen des Schelms bei Thomas Mann, Döblin,
     Brecht, Grass (Stuttgart: Kohlhammer, 1967), pp. 63-69.
884 Ziolkowski, Theodore. "Der Blick von der Irrenanstalt:
     Verrückung der Perspektive in der modernen deutschen
     Prosa." Neophilologus, 51(1967), 42-54, esp. 53-54.

1968

885 Elliot, John R., Jr. "The Cankered Muse of Günter Grass."
     Dimension, 1(1968), 516-23.
886 Emrich, Wilhelm. "Oskar Matzerath und die deutsche Poli-
     tik." Polemik. Streitschriften, Pressefehden und kriti-
     sche Essays um Prinzipien, Methoden und Massstäbe der
     Literaturkritik (Frankfurt: Athenäum, 1968), pp. 89-93.
887 Kusenberg, Kurt. "Der erste Einfall." National-Zeitung
     (Basel), 25 July 1968.
888 Maurer, Robert. "The End of Innocence: Günter Grass's
     The Tin Drum." Bucknell Review, 16, No. 2(1968), 45-65.

1969

889 Berets, Ralph Adolph. "The irrational narrator in Vir-
     ginia Woolf's The Waves, William Faulkner's The Sound and
     the Fury and Günter Grass's The Tin Drum." Diss. Uni-
     versity of Michigan, 1969. Dissertation Abstracts, 31
     (1970/71), 751A.
890 Blomster, W.V. "Oskar at the Zoppoter Waldoper." Modern
     Language Notes, 84(1969), 467-72.
891 Droste, Dietrich. "Gruppenarbeit als Mittel der Er-
     schliessung umfangreicher Romane: Grimmelshausens Aben-
     teuerlicher Simplicius Simplicissimus und Grass' Die
     Blechtrommel." Deutschunterricht, 21, No. 6(1969), 101-
     15.
892 Leroy, R. "Günter Grass, Die Blechtrommel; Hugo Claus, De
     Verwondering: Hasard où intention (suite)." Revue des
     Langues Vivantes (Bruxelles), 35(1969), 597-608; 36(1970),
     45-53.
893 O'Nan, Martha. "Günter Grass's Oskar: The rogue." The
     role of mind in Hugo, Faulkner, Beckett, and Grass (New
     York: Philosophical Library, 1969), pp. 36-48.
894 Pollmann, Leo. "Günter Grass, Die Blechtrommel." Aus der
     Werkstatt des Romans: Arithmetische Romanformeln (Stutt-
     gart: Kohlhammer, 1969), pp. 73-79.
895 Steig, Michael. "The Grotesque and the Aesthetic Response
     in Shakespeare, Dickens, and Günter Grass." Comparative
     Literature Studies (University of Illinois), 6(1969),
     167-81.
896 Ziolkowski, Theodore. Dimensions of the modern novel
     (Princeton: Princeton University Press, 1969), pp. 276-
     78, 356-57, and passim.

1970

897 Abenheimer, Karl M. "Reflections on the novel Die Blechtrommel." The philosophical journal (Edinburgh, London),
7, No. 1(1970), 37-47.
898 Boa, Elizabeth. "Günter Grass and the German Gremlin."
German Life and Letters, 23(1970), 144-51.
899 Botheroyd, Paul Francis. "Aspects of first- and third-
person narration and the problem of identity in three contemporary German-language novels: Günter Grass' Die Blechtrommel, Uwe Johnson's Das dritte Buch über Achim and Max
Frisch's Mein Name sei Gantenbein." Diss. University of
Birmingham, 1970.
900 Migner, Karl. Theorie des modernen Romans (Stuttgart:
Kröner, 1970), pp. 94-97 and passim.
901 Van Abbé, Derek. "Metamorphoses of 'Unbewältigte Vergangenheit' in Die Blechtrommel." German Life and Letters, 23(1970), 152-60.

1971

902 Diederichs, Rainer. Strukturen des Schelmischen im modernen deutschen Roman. Eine Untersuchung an den Romanen von
Thomas Mann "Bekenntnisse des Hochstaplers Felix Krull"
und Günter Grass "Blechtrommel." Diss. Zürich. Düsseldorf, Köln: Diederichs, 1971.
903 Durzak, Manfred. "Fiktion und Gesellschaftsanalyse: Die
Romane von Günter Grass." Der deutsche Roman der Gegenwart (Stuttgart: Kohlhammer, 1971), pp. 107-73.
904 Lipinsky-Gottersdorf, Hans. "Vom Ulenspiegel zum Oskar
Matzerath." Deutsche Studien, 9(1971), 154-56.
905 Mayer, Hans. "Günter Grass and Thomas Mann: Aspects of
the novel." Steppenwolf and Everyman, tr. Jack D. Zipes
(New York: Crowell, 1971), pp. 181-99.
906 Motekat, Helmut. "Zur Technik der Interpretation des
modernen Romans. Ein Versuch an Günter Grass: Die Blechtrommel." In: Ich wurde meiner Beobachtung nicht froh:
Zehn Interpretationen zu Prosatexten zeitgenössischer
Autoren. Hrsg. Goethe-Institut. Deutsch für Ausländer:
Texte zum Unterricht mit Tonbändern. Heft 1. München,
1971, pp. 42-47.
907 Plard, Henri. "Über die Blechtrommel." Text + Kritik,
No. 1/1a. 4. Aufl. (1971), pp. 27-37.
908 Seifert, Walter. "Die pikareske Tradition im deutschen
Roman der Gegenwart." Die deutsche Literatur der Gegenwart: Aspekte und Tendenzen, ed. Manfred Durzak (Stuttgart: Philipp Reclam Jun., 1971), pp. 192-210.
909 Sosnoski, M.K. "Oskar's hungry witch." Modern Fiction
Studies, 17(1971), 61-77.

1972

910 Baumgaertel, Gerhard. "Formen der Narrenexistenz in der
     deutschen Literatur der fünfziger und sechziger Jahre."
     Revue des Langues Vivantes, 38(1972), 517-26.
911 Boa, Elizabeth, and J.H. Reid. Critical strategies: Ger-
     man fiction in the twentieth century (London: Edward
     Arnold, 1972), pp. 190-94 and passim.
912 Enzweiler, Franz Rudolf. "Überlegungen zu Günter Grass
     Die Blechtrommel." Beiträge zu den Sommerkursen 1972
     (München: Goethe Institut, 1972), pp. 206-17.
913 Forys, Ryszard F. "Der Roman Die Blechtrommel von Günter
     Grass. Zwischen Tradition und Modernität." Mickiewicz-
     Blätter (Heidelberg), 1972, pp. 33-41.
914 Just, Georg. Darstellung und Appell in der "Blechtrommel"
     von Günter Grass: Darstellungsästhetik versus Wirkungs-
     ästhetik. Frankfurt: Athenäum, 1972.
915 Michelsen, Peter. "Oskar oder Das Monstrum: Reflexionen
     über Die Blechtrommel von Günter Grass." Neue Rundschau,
     83(1972), 722-40.
916 Mínguez, José Miguel. "Günter Grass y Julio Cortázar,
     Heinrich Böll y Alejo Carpentier." Boletín de estudios
     germánicos, 9(1972), 273-90.
917 Roberts, David. "Tom Thumb and the imitation of Christ.
     Towards a psycho-mythological interpretation of the 'hero'
     Oskar and his symbolic function." AULLA: Proceedings and
     papers, 14(1972), 160-74.

1973

918 Barstow, Jane Missner. "Childhood revisited and revised:
     perspective in the first person novels of Dickens, Grass
     and Proust." Diss. University of Michigan, 1973. Dis-
     sertation Abstracts International, 34(1973), 1848-A.
919 Caltvedt, Lester Norman. "Oskar Matzerath, a modern ver-
     sion of the fool: An analysis of Günter Grass' Blechtrom-
     mel." Diss. Northwestern University, 1973. Dissertation
     Abstracts International, 34(1974), 4247-A.
920 Graves, Peter J. "Günter Grass's Die Blechtrommel and
     Örtlich betäubt: the pain of polarities." Forum for
     Modern Language Studies, 9, No. 2(1973), 132-42.
921 Jung, Hans-Gernot. "Lästerungen bei Günter Grass." Süd-
     deutscher Rundfunk, 31 May 1970; rpt. Grass: Kritik--
     Thesen--Analysen, ed. Manfred Jurgensen (Bern: Francke,
     1973), pp. 75-85.
922 Just, Georg. "Die Appellstruktur der Blechtrommel."
     Grass: Kritik--Thesen--Analysen, ed. Manfred Jurgensen
     (Bern: Francke, 1973), pp. 31-43.
923 Kremer, Manfred. "Günter Grass' Die Blechtrommel und die
     pikarische Tradition." The German Quarterly, 46(1973),
     381-92.

924 Leroy, Robert. "Die Blechtrommel" von Günter Grass: Eine Interpretation. Paris: Les Belles Lettres, 1973.

925 Miles, David H. "Kafka's hapless victims and Grass's scurrilous dwarf: Notes on representative figures in the Anti-Bildungsroman." Monatshefte, 65(1973), 341-50.

926 Neis, Edgar. Günter Grass: "Die Blechtrommel." Königs Erläuterungen 159. Hollfeld: Bange, 1973.

927 Roberts, David. "Aspects of psychology and mythology in Die Blechtrommel. A study of the symbolic function of the 'hero' Oskar." Grass: Kritik—Thesen—Analysen, ed. Manfred Jurgensen (Bern: Francke, 1973), pp. 45-73.

928 Thomas, N.L. "Religious themes in the narrative works of Günter Grass (1959-68), with special reference to Die Blechtrommel." Ph.D. Diss. Salford, 1973.

1974

929 Diller, Edward. A mythic journey: Günter Grass's "Tin Drum." Lexington, Ky.: The University Press of Kentucky, 1974.

930 Fort, Deborah Charnley. "Contrast epic: a study of Joseph Heller's Catch-22, Günter Grass's The tin drum, John Barth's The sot-weed factor, and Vladimir Nabokov's Pale fire." Diss. University of Maryland, 1974. Dissertation Abstracts International, 35(1974), 3677-A.

931 Miles, David H. "The picaro's journey to the confessional: the changing image of the hero in the German Bildungsroman." PMLA, 89(1974), 980-92.

932 Mittermaier, Miriam Elise Ball. "Testing and truth: The function of the narrator in Günter Grass' Die Blechtrommel." Diss. Cornell University, 1974. Dissertation Abstracts International, 35(1974), 1114-A.

933 O'Neill, Patrick. "Musical form and the Pauline message in a key chapter of Grass's Blechtrommel." Seminar, 10 (1974), 298-307.

1975

934 Mayor, Elfriede M. "Social criticism in Günter Grass's Die Blechtrommel." Diss. University of California (Riverside), 1975. Dissertation Abstracts International, 36 (1975), 3696-A.

935 O., H. "Aus dem Erlaubnis des Blocks: Zum Tode Ludwig Gabriel Schriebers." Der Tagesspiegel, 17 April 1975, p. 4.

936 Rothenberg, Jürgen. "Anpassung oder Widerstand? Über den 'Blechtrommler' Günter Grass und sein Verhältnis zur Zeitgeschichte." Germanisch-Romanische Monatsschrift, 25 (1975), 176-98.

937 Tournier, Michel. "Le Tambour relu par Le Roi des Aulnes." Le Monde, 17 January 1975, p. 21.

1961

938 Anon. "Grass: Dingslamdei." Der Spiegel, 15(11 October 1961), 88-91.
939 B., W. "Grass spielt Katz und Maus." Nürnberger Nachrichten, 17 November 1961.
940 F., K. "Der grosse Mahlke und das Dingslamdei." Donau Zeitung (Ulm), 5 October 1961.
941 Enzensberger, Hans Magnus. "Trommelt weiter." Frankfurter Hefte, 16(1961), 860-62.
942 Fink, Humbert. "Dennoch mehr als ein Abfallprodukt." Die Presse (Wien), 19 November 1961.
943 Fischer, Gerd. "Vom Dingslamdei." Neue-Rhein-Zeitung (Essen), 7 October 1961.
944 Hartung, Rudolf. "Porträt eines Kriegshelden." Der Tagesspiegel (Berlin), 26 November 1961.
945 Hensel, Georg. "Nicht nur von der Maus gefressen." Darmstädter Echo, 18 November 1961.
946 Höller, Franz. "Das Kraftgenie aus Danzig." Ost-West-Kurier (Frankfurt/M.), October 1961.
947 Horst, Karl August. "Ferne Trommelschläge." Merkur (Köln), 15(1961), 1197-98.
948 Kaiser, Joachim. "Die Unbefangenheit des Raubtiers." Süddeutsche Zeitung (München), 7/8 October 1961.
949 Karasek, Hellmuth. "Der Knorpel am Hals." Stuttgarter Zeitung, 11 November 1961; rpt. Gert Loschütz, Von Buch zu Buch (1968), pp. 27-28.
950 Kayser, Beate. "Grass überwuchert die Stadt Danzig." Münchner Merkur, 21/22 October 1961.
951 Klunker, Heinz. "Unpathetisches Denkmal für Mahlke." Europäische Begegnung (Hannover), June 1961, pp. 56-57.
952 Korn, Karl. "Epitaph für Mahlke." Frankfurter Allgemeine Zeitung, 7 October 1961; rpt. Gert Loschütz, Von Buch zu Buch (1968), pp. 28-31.
953 Nöhbauer, Hans F. "Joachim Mahlkes Vierklee." Abendzeitung (München), 25 October 1961.
954 Nolte, Jost. "Ich schreibe, denn das muss weg." Die Welt (Hamburg), 19 October 1961; rpt. Gert Loschütz, Von Buch zu Buch (1968), pp. 31-34.
955 Rainer, Wolfgang. "Welt im Adamsapfel." Der Tag (Berlin), 3 December 1961.
956 Reich-Ranicki, Marcel. "Die Geschichte des Ritterkreuzträgers." Die Zeit, 10 November 1961, p. 19.
957 Roth, Richard R. "Im kommerziellen Kielwasser der Blechtrommel." Die Kultur (Munich), 9, No. 168(October 1961), p. 11.
958 Schlossarek, G. Dieter. "Eine Novelle von Günter Grass." Bücherkommentare, 10, No. 4(1961), 2.

959 Schüler, Gerhard. "Katz und Maus." Süd-Kurier (Konstanz), 30/31 December 1961.

960 Schwedhelm, Karl. "Danziger schweres Goldwasser." St. Galler Tagblatt, 19 November 1961.

961 von Vegesack, Thomas. "Danzig i Världslitteraturen." Stockholms Tidningen, 20 November 1961.

962 Wagenbach, Klaus. "Günter Grass: Katz und Maus." Evangelischer Literaturbeobachter (München), No. 44(December 1961), pp. 882-83.

963 Widmer, Walter. "Baal spielt Katz und Maus." National-Zeitung (Basel), 19 December 1961; rpt. Gert Loschütz, Von Buch zu Buch (1968), pp. 34-35.

964 Wolken, Karl Alfred. "Neues aus der Kaschubei." Christ und Welt (Stuttgart), 20 October 1961.

1962

965 Anon. "Nur mit der Zange anzufassen!" Das Ritterkreuz (Wiesbaden), April 1962; rpt. Loschütz, Von Buch zu Buch (1968), pp. 48-50.

966 Baranowski, W. "Das Holz, aus dem man Helden schnitzt." Das andere Deutschland (Hannover), Jan. 1962, p. 2.

967 Baumgart, Reinhard. "Günter Grass: Katz und Maus." Neue deutsche Hefte, No. 85(1962), pp. 153-54.

968 Carpelan, Bo. Hufstudstagsbladet (Helsinki), 28 December 1962.

969 Delez, Bernard. "Les lettres Allemandes." La Revue Nouvelle, 36(1962), 345-46.

970 Enzensberger, Hans Magnus. "Zusatz: Der verständige Anarchist." Einzelheiten (Frankfurt/M.: Suhrkamp, 1962), pp. 227-33.

971 Eyssen, Jürgen. "Umstrittene Bücher." Bücherei und Bildung, 14(1962), 75.

972 Frey, John R. Books Abroad, 36(Summer 1962), 295.

973 Grözinger, Wolfgang. "Der Roman der Gegenwart: Epik ohne Gesellschaft." Hochland, 54(1961/62), 169.

974 Ihlenfeld, Kurt. "Rarität und Realität." Eckart-Jahrbuch, 1961/62, pp. 278-80.

975 Maier, Wolfgang. "Moderne Novelle: Günter Grass, Katz und Maus." Sprache im technischen Zeitalter (Stuttgart), 1 (1961/62), 68-71.

976 Ottinger, Emil. "Zur mehrdimensionalen Erklärung von Straftaten Jugendlicher am Beispiel der Novelle Katz und Maus von Günter Grass." Monatsschrift für Kriminologie und Strafrechtsreform (Köln), 5/6(1962), 175-83; rpt. Gert Loschütz, Von Buch zu Buch, pp. 38-48.

977 Schauder, Karlheinz. "Ein Nachtrag zur Blechtrommel." Zeitwende, 33(1962), 339-40.

978 Segebrecht, Dietrich. "Umstrittene Bücher: Günter Grass, Katz und Maus." Bücherei und Bildung, 14(1962), 73-75.

979 Todd, Olivier. "Le chat et la souris." France Observa-
teur (Paris), 18 October 1962.
980 Wallraf, Karlheinz. "Umstrittene Bücher: Günter Grass,
Katz und Maus." Bücherei und Bildung, 14(1962), 186-87.
981 Winkler-Sölm, Oly. "Junge Literatur." Deutsche Rundschau, 88(1962), 184-85.

1963

982 Anon. Christian Century, 80(7 August 1963), 983.
983 Anon. "An outcast hero." Time, 82(23 August 1963), 75-
76.
984 Anon. "Marked man." Newsweek, 62(9 September 1963), 93-
94.
985 Barrett, William. "Odd man out." Atlantic, 212(September 1963), 122.
986 Bauke, J.P. "To be different in Danzig." Saturday Review, 46(10 August 1963), 28.
987 Bradbury, Malcolm. Punch, 245(28 August 1963), 323-24.
988 Burns, Richard K. Library Journal, 88(August 1963), 2926.
989 Cysarz, Herbert. "Verdient unsere Zeit diesen Bestseller?" Deutsche National-Zeitung und Soldatenzeitung (München), 15 November 1963.
990 Davenport, Guy. National Review, 15(8 October 1963), 313.
991 Enright, D.J. "After the dwarf." New Statesman, 66(23
August 1963), 227-28.
992 Gutwillig, Robert. "House of Mirrors." New York Herald
Tribune Books, 40(11 August 1963), 5.
993 Himmel, Hellmuth. Geschichte der deutschen Novelle.
Bern, München: Francke, 1963, pp. 487-89.
994 Hinde, Thomas. Spectator, 211(23 August 1963), 238.
995 Levine, Paul. "Easterns and Westerns." Hudson Review,
16(Autumn 1963), 455-62.
996 McGovern, Hugh. America, 109(14 September 1963), 264.
997 Murray, J.G. Critic, 22(October 1963), 77.
998 Quinn, John J. Best Seller, 23(15 August 1963), 162-63.
999 Rand, Max. Uusi Suomi (Helsinki), 5 May 1963.
1000 Spender, Stephen. New Yorker, 39(10 August 1963), 88-89.
1001 Spender, Stephen. "Beneath the adam's apple, the tin drum
beats on." New York Times Book Review, 68(11 August
1963), 5.

1964

1002 Zampa, Georgio. La Stampa (Rome), 22 January 1964.

1965

1003 Dahne, Gerhard. "Wer ist Katz und wer ist Maus?" Neues
Deutschland, No. 310, Beilage (1965); rpt. Gert Loschütz,

Von Buch zu Buch (1968), pp. 35-37.

1004 Friedrichsmeyer, Erhard M. "Aspects of myth, parody, and obscenity in Grass' Die Blechtrommel and Katz und Maus." The Germanic Review, 40(1965), 240-50.

1005 Kunkel, Francis L. "Clowns and Saviors: Two Contemporary Novels." Renascence (Milwaukee), 18, No. 1(Fall 1965), 40-44.

1006 Ottinger, Emil. "Denn was mit Katze und Maus begann, quält mich heute . . . ." Eckart-Jahrbuch, 1964/65, pp. 231-37.

1966

1007 Anon. "Das Dingslamdei." Der Spiegel, 20(26 December 1966), 22-25.

1008 Bruce, James C. "The Equivocating Narrator in Günter Grass's Katz und Maus." Monatshefte, 58(1966), 139-49.

1009 Cunliffe, W.G. "Günter Grass: Katz und Maus." Studies in Short Fiction, 3, No. 2(Winter 1966), 174-85.

1010 Lehmann, Lutz. "Der Möwenmist ist aus Gips." Die Zeit (American ed.), 16 August 1966, p. 12.

1011 Neuss, Wolfgang. "Katz und Maus und Neuss." Konkret, No. 9(1966), pp. 15-16.

1012 Ruhleder, Karl H. "A Pattern of Messianic Thought in Günter Grass' Cat and Mouse." The German Quarterly, 39 (1966), 599-612.

1013 Willis, Ronald. "On oddities." Books and Bookmen, 11 (September 1966), 44-45.

1968

1014 Behrendt, Johanna E. "Die Ausweglosigkeit der menschlichen Natur: Eine Interpretation von Günter Grass' Katz und Maus." Zeitschrift für Deutsche Philologie, 87(1968), 546-62.

1015 Edschmid, Kasimir. "Gutachten." Gert Loschütz, Von Buch zu Buch (1968), pp. 60-61.

1016 Enzensberger, Hans Magnus. "Gutachten." Gert Loschütz, Von Buch zu Buch (1968), pp. 61-64.

1017 Jens, Walter. "Gutachten." Gert Loschütz, Von Buch zu Buch (1968), pp. 64-65.

1018 Martini, Fritz. "Gutachten." Gert Loschütz, Von Buch zu Buch (1968), pp. 58-60.

1969

1019 Behrendt, Johanna E. "Auf der Suche nach dem Adamsapfel. Der Erzähler Pilenz in Günter Grass' Novelle Katz und Maus." Germanisch-romanische Monatsschrift, 50(1969), 313-26.

1020 Fulton, Edythe K. "Günter Grass's Cat and Mouse Obsession and Life." Forum (Houston), 7, No. 2(1969), 26-31.

1021 Kafka, Vladimír. "Třikrát z NSR." Listy, 2, No. 13 (1969), 11.

1022 Lohner, Edgar. "Introduction." Katz und Maus, ed. Edgar Lohner (Waltham, Mass.: Blaisdell, 1969), pp. v-xv.

1023 Lucke, Hans. "Günter Grass' Novelle Katz und Maus im Unterricht." Der Deutschunterricht, 21, No. 2(1969), 86-95.

1024 Zimmermann, Werner. "Günter Grass: Katz und Maus." Deutsche Prosadichtungen unseres Jahrhunderts. Interpretationen für Lehrende und Lernende. Band 2 (Düsseldorf: Schwann, 1969), pp. 267-300.

1970

1025 Pickar, Gertrud B. "The Aspect of Colour in Günter Grass's Katz und Maus." German Life and Letters, 23 (1970), 304-309.

1026 Schweckendiek, Adolf. "Joachim Mahlke in Günter Grass' Katz und Maus." Könnt ich Magie von meinem Pfad entfernen: Neurosenkundliche Studien an Gestalten der Dichtung (Berlin, Hans Lungwitz-Stiftung; Leimen: Marx OHG, 1970), pp. 42-47.

1027 Spaethling, Robert H. "Günter Grass: Cat and Mouse." Monatshefte, 62(1970), 141-53.

1971

1028 Fickert, Kurt J. "The Use of Ambiguity in Cat and Mouse." German Quarterly, 44(1971), 372-78.

1029 Kaiser, Gerhard. Günter Grass. Katz und Maus. Literatur im Dialog. Bd. 1. München: Fink, 1971, 52pp.

1030 Karthaus, Ulrich. "Katz und Maus von Günter Grass: eine politische Dichtung." Deutschunterricht, 23, No. 1(1971), 74-85.

1031 Neis, Edgar. Günter Grass: "Katz und Maus." Königs Erläuterungen 162. Hollfeld: Bange, 1971.

1032 Pfeiffer, John R. "Katz und Maus: Grass's debt to Augustine." Papers on language and literature (Edwardsville, Ill.), 7(1971), 279-92.

1033 Pickar, Gertrud Bauer. "Intentional ambiguity in Günter Grass's Katz und Maus." Orbis Litterarum (Copenhagen), 26(1971), 232-45.

1034 Tiesler, Ingrid. Günter Grass. "Katz und Maus." Interpretationen zum Deutschunterricht. Hrsg. Rupert Hirschenauer and Albrecht Weber. München: Oldenbourg, 1971.

1972

1035 Siegler, Wilhelm. "Die Rolle des Erzählers in der Novelle

Katz und Maus von Günter Grass." Interpretationskurse
"Moderne Literatur" auf Tonband. Inter-Nationes: Kultureller Tonbanddienst. Beilage. München: Goethe-Institut, 1972, pp. 37-42.
1036 Ziolkowski, Theodore. "The Fifth Gospels." Fictional
Transfigurations of Jesus (Princeton: Princeton U.P.,
1972), esp. pp. 238-50 and passim.

1973

1037 Croft, Helen. "Günter Grass's Katz und Maus." Seminar,
9(1973), 253-64.
1038 Thomas, N.L. "An analysis of Günter Grass' Katz und Maus
with particular reference to the religious themes." German Life and Letters, 26(April 1973), 227-38.

3 / Hundejahre (1963)

1963

1039 Anon. "Unflätiger Grass." Das Deutsche Wort (Köln), 1
September 1963.
1040 Anon. "Dogs and the deflation of demons." Times Literary
Supplement, 62(27 September 1963), 728.
1041 Anon. "Die Hundejahre des Günter Grass." Berliner Welle,
27 November 1963; rpt. Gert Loschütz, Von Buch zu Buch
(1968), pp. 98-100.
1042 Baumgart, Reinhard. "Mustermesse deutscher Prosa." Süddeutsche Zeitung, 6 July 1963, p. 5.
1043 Blöcker, Günter. "Im Zeichen des Hundes." Frankfurter
Allgemeine Zeitung, 14 September 1963.
1044 Brüdigam, Heinz. "Groteske, phantastische Gesellschafts-
kritik. Einige Bemerkungen zu den Hundejahren von Günter
Grass." Kultur und Gesellschaft, No. 10(1963), pp. 10-11.
1045 Enzensberger, Hans Magnus. "Günter Grass: Hundejahre."
Der Spiegel, 17(4 September 1963), 70-71.
1046 F., K. "Dreht euch nicht um! Der Knirscher geht um."
Schwäbische Donauzeitung (Ulm), 21 August 1963.
1047 Glaser, Hermann. "Die Hundejahre als politisches Buch."
Tribüne (Frankfurt), 2(1963), 883-86.
1048 Härtling, Peter. "Von Langfuhr in die Scheuchengrube."
Der Monat (Berlin), 15, No. 180(1963), 62-68.
1049 Häussermann, Bernhard. "Ein Buch, in dem es päsert und
funkert." Hannoversche Allgemeine, 7 September 1963.
1050 Hahnl, Hans Heinz. "Der neue Grass." Die Zukunft (Wien),
September 1963.
1051 Hartung, Rudolf. "Günter Grass: Hundejahre." Neue Rundschau (Frankfurt), 74(1963), 652-58; rpt. Gert Loschütz,
Von Buch zu Buch (1968), pp. 92-98.

1052 Herchenröder, Jan. "Das schlimme Gleichnis von den Hunde-
      jahren." Abendpost (Frankfurt), 17/18 August 1963.
1053 Hohoff, Curt. "Die Welt der Vogelscheuchen." Rheinischer
      Merkur (Köln), 15 November 1963.
1054 Horst, Karl August. "Die Vogelscheuchen des Günter
      Grass." Merkur (Köln), 17(1963), 1003-1008.
1055 Jenny, Urs. "Ein Hundetorso aus Kartoffelschalen." Die
      Weltwoche (Zürich), 4 October 1963.
1056 Jens, Walter. "Das Pandämonium des Günter Grass." Die
      Zeit, 6 September 1963; rpt. Gert Loschütz, Von Buch zu
      Buch (1968), pp. 85-89.
1057 Kabel, Rainer. "Grotesk ist zugleich auch moralisch."
      Vorwärts (Bad Godesberg), 2 October 1963.
1058 Kaiser, Joachim. "Walter Materns Hundejahre." Süddeut-
      sche Zeitung (München), 21 September 1963.
1059 Kaufmann, Harald. "Hundejahre und satirischer Weltunter-
      gang." Neue Zeit (Graz), 9 November 1963.
1060 Klein, Otto. "Die grässlichen Hundejahre." Das Deutsche
      Wort (Köln), 18 October 1963.
1061 Meckel, Eberhard. "Hundejahre." Badische Zeitung (Frei-
      burg), 30/31 December 1963.
1062 Michaelis, Rolf. "Höllenfahrt mit Günter Grass." Stutt-
      garter Zeitung, 7 September 1963, Literaturblatt, p. IV.
1063 Müller, André. "Realistisch im Detail, unrealistisch im
      Ganzen." Die Tat, 7 December 1963.
1064 Nagel, Ivan. "Günter Grass' Hundejahre." Die Zeit (Ham-
      burg), 27 September 1963, pp. 19-20.
1065 Nöhbauer, Hans F. "Die grosse Danziger Hunde-Saga."
      Abendzeitung (München), 10/11 August 1963.
1066 Nolte, Jost. "Der Zeit in den schmutzigen Rachen gegrif-
      fen." Die Welt (Hamburg), 7 September 1963.
1067 Pack, Claus. "Cave Canem." Wort und Wahrheit, 18(1963),
      714-16.
1068 Röhl, Klaus Rainer. "Bestseller auf Vorschuss." Konkret
      (Hamburg), No. 9(September 1963), pp. 23-24.
1069 Scholz, Hans. "Schildernder, bildernder Auerdichter."
      Der Tagesspiegel (Berlin), 1 September 1963.
1070 Schwedhelm, Karl. "Aus vollem Hals erzählt." St. Galler
      Tagblatt, 8 September 1963.
1071 Siering, Joachim. Neue Deutsche Hefte (Gütersloh), 10,
      No. 96(1963), 131-34.
1072 Stammen, Theo, and Dietrich Segebrecht. "Ein Hundeleben:
      Günter Grass, Hundejahre." Bücherei und Bildung, 15
      (1963), 464-67.
1073 Tank, Kurt Lothar. "Die Diktatur der Vogelscheuchen."
      Sonntagsblatt (Hamburg), 1 September 1963, p. 15.
1074 Ungureit, Heinz. "Da wären die Hundejahre." Frankfurter
      Rundschau, 31 August 1963.
1075 Vetter, Hans. "Ein Spruchkammer-Kabarett über die Hitler-
      schen Hundstage." Kölner Stadt-Anzeiger, 17/18 August
      1963.

1076 Vormweg, Heinrich. "Apokalypse mit Vogelscheuchen."
Deutsche Zeitung (Köln), 31 August 1963, p. 18; rpt. Gert
Loschütz, Von Buch zu Buch (1968), pp. 70-75.
1077 Wagenbach, Klaus. "Jens tadelt zu unrecht." Die Zeit,
20 September 1963, p. 17; rpt. Gert Loschütz, Von Buch zu
Buch (1968), pp. 89-92.
1078 Wallmann, Jürgen P. "Günter Grass: Hundejahre." Die Tat
(Zürich), 6 September 1963.
1079 Wallmann, Jürgen P. "Zeitkritik im Roman." Deutsche
Rundschau, 89, No. 12(1963), 93-96.
1080 Wiegenstein, Roland H. "Hundejahre." Westdeutscher Rundfunk (Köln), 28 October 1963; rpt. Gert Loschütz, Von
Buch zu Buch (1968), pp. 75-79.
1081 Wiegenstein, Roland H. "Noch ein Vorschlag, Günter Grass
zu verstehen." Frankfurter Hefte, 18(1963), 870-73.
1082 Wien, Werner. "Der vorbestellte Erfolg." Darmstädter
Echo, 4 October 1963.
1083 Wolken, Karl Alfred. "Bis zum Anbruch der Müdigkeit."
Christ und Welt (Stuttgart), 11 October 1963.

1964

1084 Arnold, Heinz Ludwig. "Die unpädagogische Provinz des
Günter Grass." Eckart-Jahrbuch, 1963/64, pp. 299-304;
rpt. Brauchen wir noch die Literatur? (Düsseldorf: Bertelsmann, 1972), pp. 134-37.
1085 Batt, Kurt. "Groteske und Parabel. Anmerkungen zu Hundejahre von Günter Grass und Herr Meister von Walter Jens."
Neue deutsche Literatur, 12, No. 7(1964), 57-66.
1086 Brandell, Gunnar. Svenska Dagbladet (Stockholm), 20
January 1964.
1087 Carlsson, Anni. "Der Roman als Anschauungsform der
Epoche. Bemerkungen zu Thomas Mann und Günter Grass."
Neue Zürcher Zeitung, 21 November 1964, p. 23.
1088 Grözinger, Wolfgang. "Der Roman der Gegenwart: Die Gefahr der grossen Stoffe." Hochland, 56(1963/64), 173-75.
1089 Hohoff, Curt. "Günter Grass, Hundejahre." Universitas,
19(1964), 87-90.
1090 Kafka, Vladimír. "Psí roky Güntera Grasse a Německa."
Knížní Kultura (Prague), 1, No. 2(1964), 66-67.
1091 Klunker, Heinz. "Günter Grass und seine Kritiker." Europäische Begegnung (Braunschweig), 4(1964), 466-69.
1092 Kurz, Paul Konrad. "Hundejahre: Beobachtungen zu einem
zeitkritischen Roman." Stimmen der Zeit (München), 89,
No. 1(1963/64), 107-20; rpt. Über moderne Literatur.
Standorte und Deutungen (Frankfurt: Knecht, 1967), pp.
158-76.
1093 Langfelder, Paul. Viata Romîneascâ (Bucharest), November
1964.
1094 Michalski, John. Books Abroad, 38(Summer 1964), 287-88.

1095 Steiner, George. "The Nerve of Günter Grass." <u>Commentary</u>, 37(May 1964), 77-80.
1096 Stomps, Victor Otto. "Hundejahre." RIAS (Berlin), 25 January 1964; <u>Text + Kritik</u>, No. 1, 2nd. edn. (1964), 9-12; rpt. Gert Loschütz, <u>Von Buch zu Buch</u> (1968), pp. 79-84.
1097 Ströbinger, R. "Psí roky Güntera Grasse." <u>Lidová Demo-cracie</u>, 8 March 1964, p. 5.
1098 Werner, Herbert. "Hundejahre." <u>Kirche in der Zeit</u>, 19, No. 3(1964), 122-24.

1965

1099 Anon. <u>Kirkus Service</u>, 33(15 March 1965), 337.
1100 Anon. <u>Booklist</u>, 61(1 April 1965), 740-41.
1101 Anon. "Hound of Hell." <u>Time</u>, 85(28 May 1965), 110.
1102 Anon. <u>Choice</u>, 2(September 1965), 391.
1103 Anon. "The Dog it Was." <u>Times Literary Supplement</u>, 64 (11 November 1965), 997.
1104 Anon. <u>Newsweek</u>, 66(27 December 1965), 73.
1105 Ascherson, Neal. "Danzig to Düsseldorf." <u>New Statesman</u>, 70(26 November 1965), 843-44.
1106 Brooke, Jocelyn. <u>Listener</u>, 74(9 December 1965), 969.
1107 Burns, Richard K. <u>Library Journal</u>, 90(1 June 1965), 2582.
1108 Davenport, Guy. <u>National Review</u>, 17(27 July 1965), 659.
1109 Enright, D.J. "Casting out demons." <u>New York Review of Books</u>, 4(3 June 1965), 8-10.
1110 Hill, William B. <u>Best Seller</u>, 25(1 June 1965), 116-17.
1111 Johnson, Lucy. "Grass' Fireworks." <u>Progressive</u>, 29(July 1965), 34-35.
1112 Kafka, Vladimir. "Günter Grasse album fantastických grotesek." <u>Světová literatura</u> (Prague), 10, No. 2(1965), 200-23.
1113 Klausler, Alfred P. "The Jew as Protagonist." <u>Christian Century</u>, 82(28 July 1965), 941.
1114 Klein, Marcus. "The Thirty-two Tiers of Hell." <u>Reporter</u>, 33(12 August 1965), 51-52, 54.
1115 Kluger, Richard. "Tumultuous Indictment of Man." <u>Harper's Magazine</u>, 230(June 1965), 110-13.
1116 Lindroth, James R. "Out of Hitler's Kennel." <u>America</u>, 112(26 June 1965), 903.
1117 McDonnel, T.P. <u>Critic</u>, 24(August 1965), 80.
1118 Maddocks, Melvin. "A phantom gets chased." <u>Christian Science Monitor</u>, 57(27 May 1965), 7.
1119 Maloff, Saul. <u>Commonweal</u>, 83(3 December 1965), 287.
1120 Peters, H.F., and Michael Stone. "Creator of Superior Scarecrows." <u>Saturday Review</u>, 48(29 May 1965), 25-27.
1121 Rees, Goronwy. "Gothic Masterpiece." <u>Spectator</u>, 215 (17 December 1965), 816.
1122 Roloff, Michael. "Günter Grass." <u>Atlantic</u>, 215(June 1965), 94-97.

1123 Rovit, Earl. "The Holy Ghost and the Dog." American Scholar, 34(Autumn 1965), 676-84.

1124 Ryszka, Francisek. Wspólczesność (Warsaw), 1965.

1125 Shuttleworth, Martin. Punch, 249(1 December 1965), 816.

1126 Simon, John. "And man created dog." Book Week, 2(23 May 1965), 1, 12-13.

1127 Solotaroff, Theodore. "The Brownshirt Decade." New Republic, 152(19 June 1965), 21-23.

1128 Spender, Stephen. "Scarecrows and Swastikas." New York Times Book Review, 70(23 May 1965), 1 and 32.

1129 West, Anthony. "The hound of Hitler." Newsweek, 65 (24 May 1965), 116, 118.

1130 West, Anthony. "Making scarecrows." New Yorker, 41 (20 November 1965), 236, 238, 241.

1131 West, Paul. "The grotesque purgation." Nation, 201 (16 August 1965), 81-84.

1132 Wordsworth, Christopher. "The Knife in the Water." Manchester Guardian, 93(18 November 1965), 10.

1966

1133 Anon. Kultura (Warsaw), 26 June 1966.

1134 Anon. Virginia Quarterly Review, 42(Winter 1966), xii.

1135 Bannon, Barbara G. Publisher's Weekly, 190(25 July 1966), 73.

1136 Bauke, J. Books Today, 3(5 June 1966), 9.

1137 Bense, Max. "Günter Grass, Die Hundejahre." Kritisches Jahrbuch, 1(1966), 17.

1138 Blakeston, O. Books and Bookmen, 11(January 1966), 37.

1139 Blöcker, Günter. "Günter Grass: Hundejahre." Literatur als Teilhabe: Kritische Orientierungen zur literarischen Gegenwart (Berlin: Argon Verlag, 1966), pp. 24-29.

1140 Brinkmann, Hennig. "Der komplexe Satz im deutschen Schrifttum der Gegenwart." Sprachkunst als Weltgestaltung. Festschrift für Herbert Seidler, ed. Adolf Haslinger (Salzburg, München: Pustet, 1966), pp. 13-26 (esp. 21-26).

1141 Enright, D.J. "Dog Years: Günter Grass's Third Novel." Conspirators and Poets (London: Chatto & Windus, 1966), pp. 201-207.

1142 Levay, Z. John. "The pathological muse." Modern Age, 10 (Winter 1965/66), 87-90.

1143 McGuinness, Frank. London Magazine, 5(February 1966), 83-86.

1144 Masini, Ferruccio. "Günter Grass." L'Unità (Rome), 17 September 1966.

1145 Paoli, Rudolfo. Il Tempo (Rome), 8 September 1966.

1146 Parry, Idris. "The special quality of hell." Listener, 75(3 February 1966), 173-74.

1147 Petersen, C. Books Today, 3(18 September 1966), 9.

1148 Sutton, Ellen. "Grass and Bobrowski." Times Literary Supplement, 65(17 February 1966), 123.

1967

1149 Anon. "Charakter oder Verhaltensweise--Der Mensch und die
gesellschaftlichen Verhältnisse." Literatur im Blickpunkt, ed. Arno Hochmuth (Berlin: Dietz, 1967), pp. 255-
80.
1150 Reich-Ranicki, Marcel. "Günter Grass: Hundejahre." Literatur der kleinen Schritte (Munich: Piper, 1967), pp. 22-
33; rpt. Grass: Kritik--Thesen--Analysen, ed. Manfred
Jurgensen (Bern: Francke, 1973), pp. 21-30.
1151 Steiner, George. "A note on Günter Grass." Language and
Silence (New York: Atheneum, 1967), 110-17.

1969

1152 Blomster, W.V. "The Demonic in History: Thomas Mann and
Günter Grass." Contemporary Literature, 10(1969), 75-84.
1153 Blomster, Wesley V. "The Documentation of a Novel: Otto
Weininger and Hundejahre by Günter Grass." Monatshefte,
61(1969), 122-38.
1154 Steiner, George. "Anmerkung zu Günter Grass." Sprache
und Schweigen. Essays über Sprache, Literatur und das Un-
menschliche (Frankfurt: Suhrkamp, 1969), pp. 147-55; rpt.
1973 (suhrkamp taschenbuch 123), pp. 177-85.

1970

1155 Goetze, Albrecht. "Die hundertdritte und tiefunterste
Materniade: Bemerkungen zum Roman Hundejahre von Günter
Grass anhand des Schlusskapitels." Vergleichen und Ver-
ändern. Festschrift für Helmut Motekat, ed. Albrecht
Goetze and Günther Pflaum (München: Hueber, 1970), pp.
273-77.
1156 Neuhaus, Volker. "Belle Tulla sans merci." Arcadia, 5
(1970), 278-95.
1157 Stutz, Elfriede. "Studien über Herr und Hund." Das Tier
in der Dichtung, ed. and introd. Ute Schwab (Heidelberg:
Winter, 1970), pp. 200-38.

1972

1158 Goetze, Albrecht. Pression und Deformation: Zehn Thesen
zum Roman "Hundejahre" von Günter Grass. Göppinger Ar-
beiten zur Germanistik, No. 74. Göppingen: Verlag Alfred
Kümmerle, 1972.
1159 Kurth, Lieselotte E. "Unzuverlässige Sprecher und Erzähler in deutscher Dichtung." Traditions and Transi-
tions: Studies in honor of Harold Jantz (München: Delp,
1972), pp. 105-24, esp. pp. 123-24.

1973

1160　Mason, Ann L. "Günter Grass and the Artist in history."
Contemporary Literature, 14, No. 3(1973), 347-62.
1161　Mitchell, Breon. "The demonic comedy: Dante and Grass's
Hundejahre." Papers on language and literature, 9(1973),
65-77.
1162　Šliažas, Rimvydas. "Prūsų mitologija Grasso romane Hundejahre." Aidai (New York), 1973, pp. 169-71; trans. as
"Elements of Old Prussian mythology in Günter Grass's Dog
Years." Lituanus (Chicago), 19, No. 1(1973), 39-48; and
in Baltic Literature and Linguistics, ed. Arvids Ziedonis,
Jr. et al (Columbus: Ohio State University, 1973), pp.
89-97.

1974

1163　Wehner, James Vincent. "The function of a negative myth
in Ellison's Invisible Man and in Grass's Hundejahre."
Diss. Vanderbilt University, 1974. Dissertation Abstracts
International, 35(1975), 4568-A.

4 / Örtlich betäubt (1969)

1969

1164　Anon. "Bücher: demnächst in Deutschland." Der Spiegel,
23(27 January 1969), 114.
1165　Anon. "Der neue Günter Grass: Zum Roman Örtlich betäubt."
Neue Zürcher Zeitung, 17 August 1969, p. 49.
1166　Anon. "Grass and His Nation's Burdens." Times Literary
Supplement, 25 September 1969, pp. 1077-78.
1167　Anon. "Two Novelists: (a) Günter Grass." T.L.S.: Essays
and Reviews from The Times Literary Supplement. 1969,
Vol. 8 (London: Oxford U.P., 1970), pp. 70-77.
1168　Arnold, Heinz Ludwig. "Die intellektuelle Betäubung des
Günter Grass. Zu seinem Roman Örtlich betäubt." Text +
Kritik, No. 4/4a (1969), pp. 72-76; rpt. Brauchen wir
noch die Literatur? (Düsseldorf: Bertelsmann, 1972), pp.
163-66, under title "Zeitroman mit Auslegern. Günter
Grass Örtlich betäubt"; rpt. Grass: Kritik--Thesen--Ana-
lysen, ed. Manfred Jurgensen (Bern: Francke, 1973), pp.
97-102.
1169　Becker, Hellmut. "Lehrer und Schüler in Günter Grass'
Roman Örtlich betäubt." Neue Sammlung, 9(1969), 503-10;
Moderna Språk, 65(1971), 11-20.
1170　Becker, Rolf. "Mässig mit Malzbonbons." Der Spiegel, 23
(11 August 1969), 102-103.
1171　Beckmann, Heinz. "Die Sprechblasen des Günter Grass."
Rheinischer Merkur, 15 August 1969.

1172 Braem, Helmut M. "Speckberge für Mäusefallen: Zu dem neuen Roman von Günter Grass, Örtlich betäubt." Stuttgarter Zeitung, 9 August 1969, p. 52.

1173 Clements, R.J. "European Literary Scene." Saturday Review, 52(6 December 1969), 40.

1174 Eichholz, Hildegart. "Die neue Hundeschau des Wahlhelfers Günter Grass." Münchner Merkur, 13 September 1969.

1175 Geiger, Hannsludwig. "Das Kunstgewerbliche in Herrn Grass." Evangelische Kommentare (Stuttgart), November 1969.

1176 Glaser, Hermann. "Wer ist örtlich betäubt?" Tribüne, 8 (1969), 3382-86.

1177 Höck, Wilhelm. "Der vorläufig abgerissene Faden: Günter Grass und das Dilemma des Erzählers." Hochland, 61(1969), 558-63.

1178 Hornung, Peter. "Grass: Ein ausgebrannter Fall." Deutsche Tagespost (Würzburg), 29 August 1969.

1179 Hübner, Paul. "Die Fernsehwelt im Zahnarztstuhl." Rheinische Post (Düsseldorf), 23 August 1969.

1180 Ignée, Wolfgang. "Günter Grass' belletristische Diktatur." Christ und Welt, 29 August 1969, p. 13.

1181 Kabel, Rainer. Vorwärts (Bonn), 4 September 1969.

1182 Kaiser, Joachim. "Von der Traurigkeit des Besserwissens." Süddeutsche Zeitung, 16/17 August 1969, p. 92.

1183 Karasek, Hellmuth. "Zahn gezogen." Die Zeit, 5 September 1969, p. 20.

1184 Keller, Ingeborg. "Der Skeptizismus und die Vierziger." Telegraf (Berlin), 14 August 1969.

1185 Kielinger, Thomas. "Günter Grass, Örtlich betäubt." Neue deutsche Hefte, 16, No. 4(1969), 144-49.

1186 Kirchmann, Hans. "Ein Pfeil in das trauernde Herz aller Zeitgenossen." Kölner Stadtanzeiger, 14 August 1969.

1187 Krättli, Anton. "Günter Grass und die deutsche Buchkritik." Schweizer Monatshefte, 49(1969), 753-60.

1188 Krüger, Horst. "Kein Geschmack für Ort und Augenblick." Die Zeit, 22 August 1969, p. 13.

1189 Kurz, Paul Konrad. "Örtlich betäubt oder ein Mann von vierzig Jahren." Bayerische Staatszeitung (München), 21 November 1969.

1190 Kurz, Paul K. "Das verunsicherte Wappentier: Zu Davor und Örtlich betäubt von Günter Grass." Stimmen der Zeit, 184 (1969), 374-89; rpt. Über moderne Literatur III: Standorte und Deutungen (Frankfurt: Knecht, 1971), pp. 89-112.

1191 Nolte, Jost. "Örtlich betäubt." Die Welt der Literatur, 14 August 1969, p. 3.

1192 Reich-Ranicki, Marcel. "Eine Müdeheldensosse." Die Zeit, 29 August 1969, p. 16.

1193 Ross, Werner. "Die literarische Zahnpraxis." Publik (Frankfurt), 21 November 1969.

1194 Schimansky, Gerd. "Immer neue Schmerzen. Günter Grass' Roman Örtlich betäubt." Wege zum Menschen (Göttingen),

21, No. 12(1969), 496-501.

1195 Scholz, Hans. "Pädagoge im Behandlungszimmer: ratlos."
      Der Tagesspiegel, 17 August 1969.
1196 Schwag-Felisch, Hans. "Nichts hält vor. Zu Günter Grass'
      neuem Roman Örtlich betäubt." Merkur, 23(1969), 776-79.
1197 Segebrecht, Dietrich. "Kein neues Bissgefühl." Frank-
      furter Allgemeine Zeitung, 16 August 1969.
1198 Sussdorff, Angela. "Örtlich betäubt—ein kleines Presse-
      panorama zu Günter Grass' neuestem Roman." Du (Zürich),
      29(1969), 941-46.
1199 Tank, Kurt Lothar. "Ein neuer Grass steht zur Debatte."
      Welt am Sonntag, 17 August 1969.
1200 Tank, Kurt Lothar. "Schwierigkeiten mit Grass." Sonn-
      tagsblatt, 24 August 1969, p. 22.
1201 Ungureit, Heinz. "Das Rittergestühl und der nichtver-
      brannte Hund." Frankfurter Rundschau, 6 September 1969.
1202 Wallmann, Jürgen P. "Nicht lesenswert. Günter Grass,
      Örtlich betäubt." Zeitwende, 40(1969), 774-75.
1203 Weber, Werner. "Weh, Schatten, weh . . . Günter Grass:
      Örtlich betäubt." Monat, 21, No. 253(1969), 94-98.
1204 Wessel, Kurt. Europa-Report (München), 2, No. 9(1969),
      52-53.

1970

1205 Anon. "The Dentist's Chair as an Allegory of Life."
      Time, 95(13 April 1970), 68-70.
1206 Anon. "Grass-Echo: wie ein VW." Der Spiegel, 24(4 May
      1970), 198-99.
1207 Anon. "Import duty: Günter Grass, Local Anaesthetic."
      Times Literary Supplement, 23 July 1970, p. 789.
1208 Adams, Phoebe. Atlantic Monthly, 225(April 1970), 124.
1209 Broyard, Anatole. "Günter Grass demonstrates that fiction
      is not only alive but healthier than ever." New York
      Times Book Review, 29 March 1970, pp. 1 and 15.
1210 Capouya, Emile. Saturday Review, 53(4 April 1970), 34.
1211 Davenport, Guy. National Review, 22(16 June 1970), 632-
      33.
1212 Durzak, Manfred. "Abschied von der Kleinbürgerwelt. Der
      neue Roman von Günter Grass." Basis, 1(1970), 224-37.
1213 Enright, D.J. "Always new pains." New York Review of
      Books, 14(4 June 1970), 20-23; rpt. Man is an onion: Re-
      views and essays (London: Chatto & Windus, 1972), pp. 96-
      102.
1214 Figes, Eva. "Toothache." The Listener, 84(23 July 1970),
      123-24.
1215 Friedrichsmeyer, Erhard. "The Dogmatism of Pain: Local
      Anaesthetic." Dimension, Special Issue 1970, pp. 36-49;
      rpt. A. Leslie Willson, A Günter Grass Symposium (1971),
      pp. 32-45.
1216 Gray. P.E. Yale Review, 60(Autumn 1970), p. 101.

68

1217 Haberl, Franz P. Books Abroad, 44(1970), 469; rev. and enlarged 45(1971), 115-16.

1218 Hope, Francis. "Rinse, Please." New Statesman, 80(24 July 1970), 95.

1219 Howard, Richard. Partisan Review, 37(1970), 578-79.

1220 Karasek, Hellmuth. "Örtlich anders betäubt." Die Zeit, 29 May 1970, p. 13.

1221 Kriegel, Leonard. "Günter Grass' tale of men and molars in a mended Germany." Commonweal, 92(8 May 1970), 195-96.

1222 Lindroth, James R. América, 122(23 May 1970), 564-65.

1222/1 Morse, J. Mitchell. Hudson Review, 23(Summer 1970), 329-30.

1223 O'Rourke, William. The Nation, 210(27 April 1970), 508.

1224 Park, Clara Claiborne. "To know, yet not to feel." Book World, 4(29 March 1970), p. 3.

1225 Reich-Ranicki, Marcel. "Eine Müdeheldensosse. Günter Grass: Örtlich betäubt." Lauter Verrisse (München: Piper, 1970), pp. 84-92.

1226 Shorter, Kingsley. "Günter Grass' Image-dance." The New Leader, 53(27 April 1970), 19-20.

1227 Updike, John. "View from the dental chair." New Yorker, 46(25 April 1970), 133-36.

1228 Verbeeck, Ludo. "Günter Grass tussen roman en pamflet." Dietsche Warande & Belfort, 115(1970), 677-88.

1229 Vreeland, Michael. "Grass Roots." Spectator, 225 (1 August 1970), 103-104.

1229/1 Wain, John. New Republic, 162(20 June 1970), 23-24.

1230 Wain, John. "A salute to the makers." Encounter, November 1970, p. 59.

1231 Weber, W. "Günter Grass, Örtlich betäubt." Forderungen: Bemerkungen und Aufsätze zur Literatur (Zürich, Stuttgart: Artemis Verlag, 1970), pp. 179-85.

1232 Wilson, Angus. "Molars and Incisors." Observer, 19 July 1970.

1233 Wintzen, René. "Le nouveau roman de Günter Grass." Le Monde, 6 January 1970.

1234 Wolff, G. "Killing the pain." Newsweek, 75(30 March 1970), 96.

1971

1235 Bruce, James C. "The motif of failure and the act of narrating in Günter Grass's Örtlich betäubt." Modern Fiction Studies, 17(1971), 45-60.

1236 Dencker, Klaus Peter. "Den Grass in der Schlinge." Den Grass in der Schlinge (Erlangen: VLE Verlag, 1971), pp. 50-55.

1237 Durzak, Manfred. "Plädoyer für eine Rezeptionsästhetik. Anmerkungen zur deutschen und amerikanischen Literaturkritik am Beispiel von Günter Grass' Örtlich betäubt." Akzente, 18(1971), 487-504; rpt. as "Rezeptionsästhetik als Literaturkritik," in <u>Kritik der Literaturkritik</u>, ed. Olaf Schwencke (Stuttgart: Kohlhammer, 1973), pp. 56-70.

1238 Hartl, Edwin. "Weltschmerz, dentistisch behandelt. Zu dem Roman <u>Örtlich betäubt</u> von Günter Grass." <u>Literatur und Kritik</u> (Salzburg), No. 57(1971), 433-35.

1239 Vormweg, Heinrich. "Ein weites Feld. Neuerscheinungen Herbst 1969 und Frühjahr 1970." <u>Jahresring</u> (1970/71), pp. 355-63.

1972

1240 Gössmann, Wilhelm. "Die politische Lahmlegung: <u>Örtlich betäubt</u> von Günter Grass." <u>Stimmen der Zeit</u>, 190(1972), 116-19.

1241 Reddick, John. "Action and impotence: Günter Grass's <u>Örtlich betäubt</u>." <u>Modern Language Review</u>, 67(1972), 563-78.

1242 Russell, Charles Robert. "Versions of the contemporary internalized novel: Günter Grass, William Burroughs, Max Frisch, Alain Robbe-Grillet." Diss. Cornell, 1972. <u>Dissertation Abstracts International</u>, 33(1972/73), 5746A.

1973

1243 Anon. <u>New Leader</u>, 56(29 October 1973), 15.
1244 Dawson, Helen. <u>Observer</u>, 16 December 1973, p. 29.

1974

1245 Anon. <u>Books & Bookmen</u>, 19(June 1974), 112.

5 / <u>Aus dem Tagebuch einer Schnecke</u> (1972)

1972

1246 Anon. "Forward with the gastropods." <u>Times Literary Supplement</u>, 22 December 1972, p. 1549.

1247 Beckmann, Heinz. "Mut zur Schnecke." <u>Rheinischer Merkur</u>, 1 September 1972, p. 28.

1248 Blöcker, Günter. "Wir alle sind Schnecken." <u>Süddeutsche Zeitung</u>, 26/27 August 1972, p. 109.

1249 Bondy, François. "A Snail's Eye View." <u>World</u>, 1, No. 9 (24 October 1972), 50-51.

1250 Fehrenbach, Oskar. "Grass macht sich selbst zur Schnecke." <u>Stuttgarter Zeitung</u>, 1 December 1972, p. 61.

1251 Glaser, Hermann. "Grass auf Wahlreise. Zwischen Melancholie und Utopie." <u>Tribüne</u>, 11(1972), 5016-19.

1252 Hartl, Edwin. "Im Stil von Günter Grass." <u>Die Furche</u> (Wien), 2 September 1972.

1253 Hohoff, Curt. "Der Schneckengang des Fortschritts." <u>Die</u>

Presse (Wien), 14/15 October 1972, p. V; Schwäbische Zeitung (Ravensburg), 2 November 1972.

1254 Holthusen, Hans Egon. "Deutschland, deine Schnecken." Die Welt, 24 August 1972 (Welt des Buches:), p. 1.

1255 Kielinger, Thomas. "Günter Grass, Aus dem Tagebuch einer Schnecke." Neue deutsche Hefte, 19, No. 3(1972), 155-60.

1256 Krüger, Horst. "Günter Grass / Aus dem Tagebuch einer Schnecke." Neue Rundschau, 83(1972), 741-46.

1257 Meier-Lenz, D.P. "Das 'Scheissliberale' bei Günter Grass--von Örtlich betäubt bis Tagebuch einer Schnecke." Die Horen (Hannover), 17, No. 4(1972), 74-77.

1258 Michaelis, Rolf. "Das Prinzip Zweifel." Frankfurter Allgemeine Zeitung, 2 Septbember 1972.

1259 Nolte, Jost. "Weder Geistesheld noch Wanzen: Schriftsteller." Zeitungsmagazin, 29 September 1972, p. 14.

1260 Rosenbaum, Ulrich. "Der Fortschritt als Kriechvorgang: Günter Grass und sein Schneckenbuch." Vorwärts, 10 August 1972, pp. 18-19.

1261 Schmidt, Aurel. "Die Verteidigung der Schnecke." National-Zeitung (Basel), 12 August 1972, p. III.

1262 Scholz, Günther. "Schnecken, Zweifel und Espede." Deutsche Zeitung / Christ und Welt, 8 September 1972, p. 12.

1263 Scholz, Hans. "Der Fortschritt, von Zweifel begleitet, kriecht." Der Tagesspiegel, 10 September 1972, p. 61.

1264 Schwab-Felisch, Hans. "Melancholische Variationen: Zu Günter Grass' Aus dem Tagebuch einer Schnecke." Merkur, 26(1972), 1025-30.

1265 Wallmann, Jürgen P. "Grass als Schnecke." Die Tat, 26 August 1972, p. 25.

1266 Zimmer, Dieter E. "Kriechspur des Günter Grass." Die Zeit, 29 September 1972 (Literaturbeilage:), pp. 1-2.

1973

1267 Anon. Kirkus Reviews, 41(15 July 1973), 769.
1268 Anon. Publishers Weekly, 204(23 July 1973), 62.
1269 Anon. Library Journal, 98(July 1973), 2157.
1270 Anon. National Observer, 12(13 October 1973), 19.
1271 Anon. Booklist, 70(15 November 1973), 320.
1272 Anon. New York Times Book Review, 2 December 1973, p. 75.
1273 Anon. Book World, 7(9 December 1973), 1.
1274 Adams, Phoebe. Atlantic Monthly, 232(October 1973), 130.
1275 Allen, Bruce. Library Journal, 98(1 September 1973), 2462.
1276 Ascherson, Neal. New York Review of Books, 20(1 November 1973), 10.
1277 Bell, Pearl K. "Of mollusks and men." New Leader, 29 October 1973, pp. 15-16.
1278 Coogan, Daniel. America, 129(29 September 1973), 220.
1279 Eriksson, Göran R. "I snigelns tecken." Västerbottens-Kuriren (Umeå), 13 February 1973.

1280 Fyne, Robert. Christian Century, 90(19 December 1973),
       1258.

1281 Gallant, Mavis. "How to cook cow's udder." New York
       Times Book Review, 30 September 1973, p. 5.

1282 Hingst, Wolfgang. "Schneckenprozess." Frankfurter Hefte,
       28(1973), 143-44.

1283 Kurz, Paul Konrad. "Exempla politica im Roman: Die epi-
       sierte Wahlreise." Über moderne Literatur IV: Standorte
       und Deutungen (Frankfurt: Josef Knecht, 1973), pp. 69-78.

1284 Maddocks, Melvin. Time, 102(8 October 1973), 109.

1285 Mirsky, Mark Jay. Book World, 23 September 1973, pp. 1,
       8-9.

1286 Phillipson, J.S. Best Sellers, 33(1 October 1973), 301.

1287 Raddatz, Fritz J. "Der Weltgeist als berittene Schnecke:
       Günter Grass' kleine Hoffnung--aus grosser Melancholie."
       Grass: Kritik--Thesen--Analysen, ed. Manfred Jurgensen
       (Bern: Francke, 1973), pp. 191-97.

1288 Reed, John. Christian Science Monitor, 65(26 September
       1973), 11.

1289 Schauder, Karlheinz. Neues Forum, 20(1973), 60.

1290 Schmolze, Gerhard. "Zuviele Schnecken, zuviele Kinder?"
       Zeitwende, 44(1973), 65-66.

1291 Updike, John. "Snail on the stump." New Yorker, 49(15
       October 1973), 182-85.

1292 Washburn, Martin. The Village Voice, 25 October 1973,
       p. 33.

       1974

1293 Anon. Choice, 10(January 1974), 1724.

1294 Anon. Nation, 218(16 March 1974), 343.

1295 Anon. Guardian Weekly, 110(25 May 1974), 22.

1296 Anon. Contemporary Review, 225(July 1974), 45.

1297 Anon. Prairie Schooner, 48(Fall 1974), 272.

1298 Ackroyd, Peter. The Spectator, 18 May 1974, p. 614.

1299 Enright, D.J. "On the trail of Günter Grass." Listener,
       91(6 June 1974), 737-38.

1300 Morgan, John. "Melancholy Grass." New Statesman, 87
       (7 June 1974), 809.

1301 Riedl, Joachim. Literatur und Kritik, No. 81(1974), pp.
       58-59.

1302 Robbins, Richard. "A writer's progress." Dissent, 21
       (Summer 1974), 459-60.

1303 Wilson, Angus. "Progress down the middle." Observer,
       12 May 1974, 37.

1304 Anon. "Grass und die Köchinnen." Der Spiegel, 29 (10 March 1975), 124.
1305 Anon. "Günter Grass baut Klöster." Mannheimer Morgen, 15 September 1975.
1306 Anon. "Die poetische Kraft des Kulinarischen: Günter Grass las im Hechtplatz-Theater." Die Tat (Zürich), 21 October 1975.
1307 Berg, Birgit. "Blechtrommler in der Hexenküche." Die Zeit, 14 March 1975, p. 20.
1308 Franz, Monika. "Die Küchen-Diplomatie der dicken Gret: Günter Grass las in Mannheim aus seinem neuen Buch." Rhein-Neckar-Zeitung, 15 September 1975.
1309 Kraft, Martin. "Das Fressen, das auch nur Angst ist." Neue Zürcher Zeitung, 22 October 1975.
1310 Linder, Gisela. "Günter Grass und die Köchinnen." Schwäbische Zeitung, 3 March 1975.
1311 s.s. "Werkstatteinblicke: Günter Grass las in Heidelberg aus dem Manuskript--Eine Weltchronik des Kochens ist im Entstehen." Rhein-Neckar-Zeitung, 16 October 1975.
1312 Werth, Wolfgang. "Die kochende Neunfaltigkeit." Süddeutsche Zeitung, 4 March 1975, p. 15.

IV. D R A M A

0. The Drama in general

1962

1313 Kesting, Marianne. "Günter Grass: Absurde Szenerie." Panorama des zeitgenössischen Theaters (München: Piper, 1962), pp. 253-55; revised version in 2nd. edition (München: Piper, 1969), pp. 300-304.
1314 Völker, Klaus. "Das Phänomen des Grotesken im neueren deutschen Drama." Sinn oder Unsinn? Das Groteske im modernen Drama, ed. Reinhold Grimm, Willy Jäggi, Hans Oesch (Basel: Basilius Presse, 1962), pp. 10-46.

1963

1315 Jahnke, Jürgen. "Günter Grass als Stückeschreiber." Text + Kritik, No. 1(1963), 14-16.
1316 Kesting, Marianne. "Günter Grass als Dramatiker." Welt und Wort, 18(1963), 270.

1966

1317   Esslin, Martin. "Günter Grass." The Theatre of the
        Absurd (London: Eyre & Spottiswodde, 1966), pp. 202-203.

        1967

1318   Esslin, Martin. "Introduction." In Günter Grass, Four
        Plays (New York: Harcourt, Brace and World, 1967), pp.
        vii-xii; (Harmondsworth: Penguin Books, 1972), pp. 7-13.
1319   Willson, A. Leslie. "Introduction." Hochwasser and Noch
        zehn Minuten bis Buffalo, ed. A. Leslie Willson (New York:
        Appleton-Century-Crofts, 1967), pp. 1-10.

        1970

1320   Cunliffe, W.G. "Grass and the Denial of Drama." Dimen-
        sion, Special Issue 1970, pp. 64-74; rpt. A. Leslie Will-
        son, A Günter Grass Symposium (1971), pp. 60-70.

        1971

1321   Bachmann, Claus-Henning. "Günter Grass und die schwie-
        rige Vernunft." Schwäbische Zeitung, 26 April 1971.
1322   Kaiser, Joachim. "Die Theaterstücke des Günter Grass."
        Text + Kritik, No. 1/1a, 4. Aufl. (1971), pp. 52-66.
1323   Szumowska, Henryka. "Günter Grass--Der Dramatiker."
        Studia Germanica Posnaniensia, 1(1971), 85-90.

        1972

1324   Esslin, Martin. "Günter Grass als Dramatiker." Jenseits
        des Absurden: Aufsätze zum modernen Drama (Wien: Europa-
        verlag, 1972), pp. 154-59.
1325   Yowell, Robert L. "Pre-production analyses of selected
        non-realistic plays of Günter Grass in their English
        translations." Diss. Bowling Green State University,
        1972. Dissertation Abstracts International, 33(1972/73),
        2547-A.

        1 / Onkel, Onkel (1958)

        1957

1326   Kaiser, Joachim. "Zehn Jahre Gruppe 47." Frankfurter
        Allgemeine Zeitung, 2 October 1957.

        1958

1327   Husson, Albert. "Zweimal verhinderter Mord." Theater
        Rundschau (Bonn), April 1958; rpt. Gert Loschütz, Von

Buch zu Buch (1968), pp. 113-14.

1328 Luyken, Sonja. "Onkel, Onkel." Mannheimer Morgen, 6
March 1958; rpt. Gert Loschütz, Von Buch zu Buch (1968),
pp. 112-13.

1961

1329 F. "Mörder und sein Publikum." Göttinger Presse, 1 June
1961; rpt. Gert Loschütz, Von Buch zu Buch (1968), pp.
114-16.
1330 Schüler, Gerhard. "Onkel, Onkel." Göttinger Tageblatt,
1 June 1961; rpt. Gert Loschütz, Von Buch zu Buch (1968),
pp. 116-18.

1962

1331 K., F. "Ein Prosit der Geschmacklosigkeit." Neues Öster-
reich (Wien), 20 October 1962; rpt. Gert Loschütz, Von
Buch zu Buch (1968), pp. 119-20.
1332 Kaiser, Joachim. "Böse Kinder bleiben siegreich." Süddeutsche Zeitung (München), 14 February 1962; rpt. Gert
Loschütz, Von Buch zu Buch (1968), pp. 118-19.

1965

1333 Anon. "German concerns." Times Literary Supplement, 64
(27 May 1965), 410.

1966

1334 E., K. "Onkel, Onkel." Stuttgarter Zeitung, 16 March
1966; rpt. Gert Loschütz, Von Buch zu Buch (1968), pp.
120-21.

1975

1335 Nowlan, David. "Onkel, Onkel." The Irish Times (Dublin),
14 May 1975, p. 11.
1336 Colgan, Gerry. "Clowns and Criminals." Hibernia (Dublin), 30 May 1975, p. 26.

2 / "Noch zehn Minuten bis Buffalo" (1958)

1960

1337 Kaiser, Joachim. "Günter Grass' Lokomotiven-Poesie."
Süddeutsche Zeitung (München), 23 February 1960.

1965

1338 Luft, Friedrich. "Günter Grass, Noch zehn Minuten bis
      Buffalo." Stimme der Kritik: Berliner Theater seit 1945
      (Velber bei Hannover: Friedrich Verlag, 1965), pp. 299-
      300.

      3 / Hochwasser (1960)

      1956

1339 Hornung, Peter. "Was man erlebt, wenn man zu jungen Dich-
      tern fährt" (Gruppe 47 meeting at Niederpöcking). Neue
      Presse (Passau), 16 November 1956.
1340 Schwab-Felisch, Hans. "Dichter auf dem 'elektrischen
      Stuhl'" (Gruppe 47 meeting at Niederpöcking). Frankfurter
      Allgemeine Zeitung, 1 November 1956.

      1957

1341 Meurer, Adolph. "Der Danziger Günter Grass--Uraufführung:
      Hochwasser." Ostdeutsche Monatshefte (Danzig/Berlin), 23,
      No. 6(1957), 376.

      1960

1342 Ni. "Grass: Hochwasser." Generalanzeiger der Stadt
      Wuppertal, 8 February 1960.

      1964

1343 Karsch, W. "Für Bühne und Funk." Tagesspiegel (Berlin),
      2 February 1964.
1344 Volbach, Walther R. Books Abroad, 38(Summer 1964), 287.

      1971

1345 Dixon, Christa K. "Ernst Barlach: Die Sündflut und Günter
      Grass: Hochwasser. Ein Beitrag zum Vergleich." German
      Quarterly, 44(1971), 360-71.

      4 / "Die bösen Köche" (1961)

      1961

1346 Anon. "In der Küche." Der Spiegel, 15(1 March 1961),
      77-78.
1347 Fiedler, Werner. "Der Rest ein dunkles Sösschen." Der
      Tag (Berlin), 18 February 1961; rpt. Gert Loschütz, Von
      Buch zu Buch (1968), pp. 127-28.
1348 Grack, Günther. "Fünf Gänge, die nicht sättigen." Der

Tagesspiegel (Berlin), 18 February 1961; rpt. Gert Loschütz, Von Buch zu Buch (1968), pp. 128-30.

1349 Luft, Friedrich. "Hier macht die Logik fröhlich Hand-
stand." Die Welt (Hamburg), 18 February 1961; rpt. Gert
Loschütz, Von Buch zu Buch (1968), pp. 125-27.

1350 Luft, Friedrich. "Fröhlich-frecher Umgang mit dem Ab-
surden." Die Welt (Hamburg), 21 February 1961.

1351 Niehoff, Karena. "Die bösen Köche." Süddeutsche Zeitung
(München), 18 February 1961; rpt. Gert Loschütz, Von Buch
zu Buch (1968), pp. 123-25.

1352 Pörtner, Paul (ed.). "Nachwort." Modernes deutsches
Theater 1 (Neuwied, Berlin: Luchterhand, 1961), pp. 248-
57.

1353 Urbach, Ilse. "Scharfes Süppchen von Günter Grass." Der
Kurier (Berlin), 17 February 1961; rpt. Gert Loschütz,
Von Buch zu Buch (1968), pp. 122-23.

1965

1354 Luft, Friedrich. "Günter Grass, Die bösen Köche." Stimme der Kritik: Berliner Theater seit 1945 (Velber bei
Hannover: Friedrich Verlag, 1965), pp. 300-302.

1966

1355 Spycher, Peter. "Die bösen Köche von Günter Grass--ein
'absurdes' Drama?" Germanisch-Romanische Monatsschrift,
47(1966), 161-89.

1967

1356 Bremer, Robert. "Demaskierung vor Mitternacht." Die Aufbau (New York), 26 January 1967.

1357 Davis, James. "Wicked cooks made of poor play recipe."
New York Daily News, 24 January 1967.

1358 Gilman, Richard. "Spoiling the Broth." Newsweek, 69
(6 February 1967), 106.

1359 Kerr, Walter. "Wicked Cooks by Günter Grass opens." New
York Times, 24 January 1967.

1360 Nadel, Norman. "Grass work brutal, cruel." New York
World Journal Tribune, 24 January 1967.

1361 Oliver, Edith. New Yorker, 42(4 February 1967), 93-94.

1362 Smith, William James. "Soup to Nuts: The Stage." Commonweal, 85(17 February 1967), 567.

1363 von Berg, Robert. "Die Kunst, eine Suppe zu versalzen."
Die Tat (Zürich), 4 February 1967; rpt. Gert Loschütz,
Von Buch zu Buch (1968), pp. 130-31.

1364 Watts, Richard, Jr. "The conspiracy of the cooks." New
York Post, 24 January 1967.

5 / "Eine öffentliche Diskussion" (1963)

1365 Wirsing, Sibylle. "Diskussion als Folterung." Der Tagesspiegel (Berlin), 11 February 1968, p. 4.

6 / "Goldmäulchen" (1964)

1963

1366 Kaiser, Joachim. "Theater-Tagebuch." Der Monat, 17, No.
193(1963), 55-63.

1964

1367 Braun, Hanns. "Goldmäulchen-Dialoge." Christ und Welt,
10 July 1964.
1368 Jenny, Urs. "Hundejahre auf der Bühne." Stuttgarter
Zeitung, 3 July 1964.
1369 Stauch-von Quitzow, Wolfgang. ". . . und kein Beifall für
Goldmäulchen." Sonntagsblatt, 19 July 1964.

7 / Die Plebejer proben den Aufstand (1966)

1965

1370 Anon. "Grass: Aufstand der Plebejer." Der Spiegel, 19
(15 December 1965), 127-28.

1966

1371 Anon. "In der Sackgasse des Antikommunismus." Der Morgen (Berlin), 21 January 1966; rpt. Gert Loschütz, Von
Buch zu Buch (1968), pp. 144-45.
1372 Anon. "Brot und Bier." Der Spiegel, 20(24 January 1966),
81.
1373 Anon. Kirkus Service, 34(15 September 1966), 1033.
1374 Atkinson, Brooks. Saturday Review, 49(31 December 1966),
26-27.
1375 Augstein, Rudolf. "William Shakespeare, Bertolt Brecht,
Günter Grass." Der Spiegel, 20(24 January 1966), 83-87.
1376 Baecker, Sigurd. "Vier Akte Zaudern." Vorwärts (Bonn),
16 February 1966.
1377 Baumgart, Reinhard. "Plebejer-Spätlese." Neue Rundschau
(Frankfurt), 77(1966), 335-39; rpt. Gert Loschütz, Von
Buch zu Buch (1968), pp. 149-53.
1378 Beer, K.W. "Ein Trauerspiel. Der 17. Juni des Günter
Grass." Die politische Meinung, 11, No. 3(1966), 8-9.
1379 Bentley, Eric. "In Bahnhof Friedrichstrasse." Partisan

Review, 33(1966), 97-109.

1380 Blaha, Paul. "Glanz und Elend des Intellektuellen." Der Kurier (Berlin), 16 May 1966, p. 12.

1381 Bondy, François. "Günter Grass et son Brecht-Coriolan-Galilée." Preuves, No. 181(March 1966), pp. 68-70.

1382 Brunelli, Vittorio. "Autopsy of an Insurrection." Atlas, 11(April 1966), pp. 249-50.

1383 Delmas, Eugene. "Ein deutsches Trauerspiel um Bertolt Brecht." Frankfurter Neue Presse, 18 January 1966.

1384 Dieckmann, Jörg. "National erregt, Staatstheater Karlsruhe." Theater heute, 7, No. 8(1966), p. 42.

1385 Eichholz, Armin. "Dabeisein oder nicht dabeisein." Münchner Merkur, 17 January 1966.

1386 Enright, D.J. "Kindly shoot above the trees." New York Review of Books, 7(29 December 1966), 7.

1387 Habernoll, Kurt. "Unpolitisches Theater in politischer Kaschierung." Vorwärts (Bonn), 16 February 1966.

1388 Hahnl, Hans Heinz. "Auf dem Weg zum Zeitstück unserer Misere." Arbeiter Zeitung (Wien), 17 May 1966.

1389 Hahnl, Hans Heinz. "Die Fragwürdigkeit der Eliten. Zur Burgtheateraufführung von Die Plebejer proben den Aufstand von Günter Grass." Zukunft (Wien), No. 11(1966), pp. 23-24.

1390 Hamm, Peter. "Vergeblicher Versuch, einen Chef zu entmündigen." Frankfurter Hefte, 21(1966), 206-208.

1391 Hartmann, Rainer. "Ein Trauerspiel vom deutschen Trauerspiel." Frankfurter Neue Presse, 11 July 1966; rpt. Gert Loschütz, Von Buch zu Buch (1968), pp. 154-56.

1392 Hartmann, Rainer. "Günter Grass, Die Plebejer proben den Aufstand." Tribüne, 5(1966), 2066-68.

1393 Hecht, Werner. "Brecht und die Ignoranten." Theater der Zeit, 21, No. 7(1966), 17.

1394 Hildebrandt, Dieter. "Brecht und der Rasen." Frankfurter Allgemeine Zeitung, 17 January 1966; rpt. Gert Loschütz, Von Buch zu Buch (1968), pp. 140-44.

1395 Hoffmann, Jens. "Frei nach Büchner: Günter Grass und der 17. Juni." Christ und Welt, 21 January 1966, p. 19.

1396 Hübner, Paul. "Grass kratzt am Brecht-Mythos." Rheinische Post (Duisburg), 17 January 1966.

1397 Ignée, Wolfgang. "Die Wahrheit ist konkret." Christ und Welt (Stuttgart), 21 January 1966, p. 19.

1398 Jenny, Urs. "Grass probt den Aufstand." Süddeutsche Zeitung (München), 17 January 1966; rpt. Gert Loschütz, Von Buch zu Buch (1968), pp. 135-40.

1399 Kahl, Kurt. "Nicht Brecht ist der Chef." Theater heute, 7, No. 7(1966), 35-37.

1400 Kaiser, Joachim. "Uraufführungstagebuch." Der Monat, 17, No. 210(1966), 59-71.

1401 Kersten, Hans Ulrich. "Grass versus Brecht." Basler Nachrichten, 19 January 1966.

1402 Kienzl, Florian. "Aufstand gegen die Brecht-Legende."

       Die Presse (Wien), 18 January 1966.
1403   Kitching, Jessie. Publishers Weekly, 190(26 September
       1966), 132.
1404   Klotz, Volker. "Ein deutsches Trauerspiel." Frankfurter
       Rundschau, 17 January 1966; rpt. Gert Loschütz, Von Buch
       zu Buch (1968), pp. 132-35.
1405   Konrad, H. "Dramatische Dienstleistung auf 'drittem
       Weg'." Neues Deutschland, No. 15, 1966.
1406   Kotschenreuther, Hellmut. "Der Intellektuelle in der
       Diktatur." Mannheimer Morgen, 17 January 1966.
1407   Leiser, Erwin. "Brecht, Grass und der 17. Juni 1953."
       Die Weltwoche (Zürich), 11 February 1966.
1408   Luft, Friedrich. "Ein Wallenstein der Revolution." Die
       Welt (Hamburg), 17 January 1966.
1409   Mayer, Hans. "Komödie, Trauerspiel, deutsche Misere."
       Theater heute, 7, No. 3(1966), 23-26.
1410   Mühlberger, Josef. "Bert Brecht als opportunistischer
       Modellfall. Zur Wiener Erstaufführung der Plebejer von
       Grass." Berichte des österreichischen Forschungsinsti-
       tutes für Wirtschaft und Politik (Salzburg), 21, No. 1031
       (1966), 15.
1411   Mühlberger, Josef. "Grass contra Brecht." Welt und Wort,
       21(1966), 45.
1412   Müller, André. "Ein Anti-Grass-Stück." Arbeitskreis
       Bertolt Brecht (Köln), Nachrichtenbrief 35, 1966, pp. 4-6.
1413   Nössig, Manfred. "Gott, war das schlecht." Theater der
       Zeit (Berlin-Ost), 21, No. 5(1966), 21-22.
1414   Orzechowski, Lothar. "Kein Aufstand in der Ruine." Hes-
       sische Allgemeine (Kassel), 11 July 1966.
1415   Patera, Paul. "Grass mot Brecht." Horisont (Vasa), 13,
       No. 3(1966), 80, 83.
1416   Popkin, Henry. "Mr. Brecht over a big barrel." Life, 60
       (18 February 1966), 17.
1417   Rachow, Louis A. Library Journal, 91(15 November 1966),
       5641.
1418   Reich-Ranicki, Marcel. "Trauerspiel von einem deutschen
       Trauerspiel." Die Zeit (Hamburg), 21 January 1966, pp.
       9-10.
1419   Rischbieter, Henning. "Grass probt den Aufstand."
       Theater heute (Hannover), 7, No. 2(1966), 13-16.
1420   Röhl, Klaus Rainer. "War Brecht Sozialdemokrat?" Kon-
       kret (Hamburg), No. 2(February 1966), p. 35.
1421   Schimming, W. "Die Plebejer proben den Aufstand." All-
       gemeine Zeitung (Mainz), 15 January 1966.
1422   Schlocker, Georges. "Une pièce de Günter Grass." Lettres
       Nouvelles, March-April 1966, pp. 136-39.
1423   Schott, Webster. "Out of the Nazi ash heap." New York
       Times Book Review, 71(20 November 1966), 4.
1424   Schüler, Alfred. "Coriolan und Stalinallee." Die Welt-
       woche (Zürich), 21 January 1966.

1425 Schwab-Felisch, Hans. "Günter Grass und der 17. Juni." Merkur (Köln), 20(1966), 291-94; rpt. Gert Loschütz, Von Buch zu Buch (1968), pp. 145-49.

1426 Tank, Kurt Lothar. "Ein deutsches Trauerspiel--durchgerechnet von Günter Grass." Sonntagsblatt (Hamburg), 23 January 1966, p. 20.

1427 Triesch, Manfred. "Günter Grass: Die Plebejer proben den Aufstand." Books Abroad, 40(1966), 285-87.

1428 Urbach, Ilse. "Der Aufstand tritt auf der Stelle." Der Kurier (Berlin), 17 January 1966.

1429 Werner, Herbert. "Günter Grass und der 17. Juni 1953." Kirche in der Zeit, 21(1966), 229-31.

1430 Wimmer, Ernst. "Warum das Burgtheater ausgerechnet Grass spielt." Die Wahrheit (Graz), 10 February 1966.

1431 Zwerenz, Gerhard. "Brecht, Grass und der 17. Juni. Elf Anmerkungen." Theater heute (Hannover), 7, No. 3(1966), 24.

1967

1432 Anon. Booklist, 63(15 February 1967), 612.

1433 Anon. Choice, 4(June 1967), 425.

1434 Anon. "Rome in Berlin." Times Literary Supplement, 66 (28 December 1967), 1260.

1435 Berger, Friedrich. "Es lohnt doch, mit Grass den Aufstand zu proben." Kölner Stadtanzeiger, 16 January 1967; rpt. Gert Loschütz, Von Buch zu Buch (1968), pp. 156-57.

1436 Ewen, Frederic. "Alas, poor Bertolt Brecht." Nation, 204(13 February 1967), 213-14.

1437 Ide, Heinz. "Die Geschichte und ihre Dramatiker. Coriolan als Thema für Shakespeare, Brecht und Günter Grass." Jahrbuch der schlesischen Friedrich-Wilhelms-Universität zu Breslau, Beiheft 7(1967), pp. 121-43.

1438 Kaiser, Joachim. "Grass überfordert seinen Hamlet." Süddeutsche Zeitung (München), 27 April 1967, p. 14.

1439 Karasek, Helmuth. "Beispiele für das Theater 1966." Jahresring (Stuttgart: Deutsche Verlags Anstalt), 1966/67, pp. 349-58.

1440 Reich-Ranicki, Marcel. "Günter Grass: Die Plebejer proben den Aufstand." Literatur der kleinen Schritte (München: Piper, 1967), pp. 173-78.

1441 Roloff, Michael. Commonweal, 86(19 May 1967), 266-67.

1442 Schwab-Felisch, Hans. "Zweimal Zeitgeschichte in Düsseldorf." Süddeutsche Zeitung, 25 January 1967.

1443 Stocker, Karl. "Günter Grass: Die Plebejer proben den Aufstand. Ein Diskussionsbeitrag zu einem umstrittenen Stücke." Blätter für den Deutschlehrer, 11(1967), 65-73.

1444 Vielhaber, Gerd. "Günter Grass und die Folgen." Frankfurter Allgemeine Zeitung, 19 January 1967; rpt. Gert Loschütz, Von Buch zu Buch (1968), pp. 157-59.

1445 Wendt, Ernst. "Sein grosses Ja bildet Sätze mit kleinem

Nein." Theater heute, 8, No. 4(1967), 6-11.

1968

1446 French, Philip. "Gone to Grass." New Statesman, 75(16 February 1968), 215.
1447 Hermann, Walter M. "Schuldbewusst klage ich euch an!" Hamburger Abendblatt, 5 January 1968.
1448 Hewes, Henry. "Grass on Brecht." Saturday Review, 51 (14 September 1968), 117.
1449 Nolte, Jost. "Die Plebejer proben den Aufstand." Die Welt (Hamburg), 6 January 1968; rpt. Gert Loschütz, Von Buch zu Buch (1968), pp. 159-61.

1969

1450 James, Norman. "The Fusion of Pirandello and Brecht in Marat/Sade and The Plebeians Rehearse the Uprising." Educational Theatre Journal, 21(1969), 426-38.
1451 Kuczynski, Jürgen. "Günter Grass, Die Plebejer proben den Aufstand--oder: Der Kleinbürger versucht die Macht abzugeben." Gestalten und Werke. Soziologische Studien zur deutschen Literatur (Berlin: Aufbau, 1969), pp. 341-49.

1970

1452 Bryden, Ronald. "Germany's tragedy." The Observer Review (London), 26 July 1970.
1453 Castein, Hanne. "Grass verärgert London." Die Zeit, 14 August 1970, p. 20.
1454 Elsom, John. "The English prepare Gunter Grass." London Magazine, 10(October 1970), 81-86.
1455 Grimm, Reinhold. "Spiel und Wirklichkeit in einigen Revolutionsdramen." Basis, 1(1970), 49-93 (Die Plebejer proben den Aufstand: 66-67).
1456 Hayman, Ronald. "Underneath the table." The Times (London), 18 July 1970, p. 7.
1457 Hunt, Albert. "Escaping to Freedom." New Society, 6 August 1970, pp. 252-53.

1971

1458 Bindzau, Rainer. "Bertolt Brecht bei Günter Grass." Trebetygsuppsats. University of Stockholm, 1971.
1459 Grathoff, Dirk. "Dichtung versus Politik: Brechts Coriolan aus Günter Grassens Sicht." Brecht heute-Brecht today, 1(1971), 168-87.
1460 Redmond, James. "Günter Grass: a Kashubian G.B.S." Modern Drama (Lawrence, Kansas), 14(1971), 104-13.
1461 Redmond, James. "Günter Grass und 'Der Fall Brecht'." Modern Language Quarterly, 32(1971), 387-400.

1462 Wirth, Andrzej. "Günter Grass and the Dilemma of Documentary Drama." Dimension, Special Issue 1970, pp. 22-35; rpt. A. Leslie Willson, A Günter Grass Symposium (1971), pp. 18-31.

1972

1463 Melchinger, Siegfried. "Interpretation des Stückes: Die Plebejer proben den Aufstand von Günter Grass." Ich er- nenne gewisse Dinge für falsch: Zehn Interpretationen zu Theaterstücken und Hörspielen zeitgenössischer Autoren. Hrsg. Goethe-Institut, Deutsch für Ausländer: Texte zum Unterricht mit Tonbändern. Heft 2. München, 1972, pp. 43-49.

1464 Seiler, Bernd W. "Exaktheit als ästhetische Kategorie: Zur Rezeption des historischen Dramas der Gegenwart." Poetica, 5(1972), 388-433, esp. 391-92.

1973

1465 Brown, Thomas K. "'Die Plebejer' und Brecht: An interview with Günter Grass." Monatshefte (Wisconsin), 65, No. 1 (1973), 5-13.

1466 Brunkhorst, Martin. "Das Experiment mit Coriolanus: Günter Grass." Shakespeares 'Coriolanus' in deutscher Be- arbeitung (Berlin, New York: Walter de Gruyter, 1973), pp. 138-56.

1467 Hughes, Catherine. "The plebeians rehearse the uprising." Plays, politics, and polemics (New York: Drama Book Specialists/Publishers, 1973), pp. 175-81.

1468 Metzger, Lore. "Günter Grass's rehearsal play." Con- temporary Literature, 14, No. 2(1973), 197-212.

8 / "The World of Günter Grass" (1966)

1469 Chapin, Louis. "World of Günter Grass." Christian Science Monitor, 2 May 1966.

1470 Cooke, Richard P. "German author on stage." Wall Street Journal, 28 April 1966.

1471 Kauffmann, Stanley. "The world of Günter Grass." New York Times, 27 April 1966.

1472 Oliver, Edith. New Yorker, 42(7 May 1966), 120.

1473 Pasolli, Robert. Nation, 202(16 May 1966), 597-98.

1474 Silver, Lee. "There is much talk in Günter Grass' world." New York Daily News, 27 April 1966.

1475 Watts, Richard, Jr. "An evening with Günter Grass." New York Post, 27 April 1966.

9 / <u>Four Plays</u> (1967)

1967

1476 Anon. <u>Kirkus Service</u>, 35(15 January 1967), 105.
1477 Anon. <u>Booklist</u>, 63(15 May 1967), 977.
1478 Gregory, Sister M. <u>Best Seller</u>, 27(15 April 1967), 37.
1479 Mander, John. "Reality beyond realism." <u>Book Week</u>, 4 (21 May 1967), 12.
1480 Rachow, Louis A. <u>Library Journal</u>, 92(1 April 1967), 1508.

1968

1481 Wood, M. <u>Observer</u>, 3 March 1968, p. 23.

10 / "Die Vogelscheuchen" (1970)

1482 Anon. "Grass--süsses Adagio." <u>Spiegel</u>, 24(12 October 1970), 256.
1483 Geitel, Klaus. "Ein Märchen aus uralten Tagen. Vogelscheuchen-Ballett von Reimann/Grass uraufgeführt." <u>Die Welt</u>, 9 October 1970, p. 23.
1484 Kotschenreuther, Hellmut. "Eine Allegorie des Terrors." <u>Die Zeit</u>, 16 October 1970, p. 27.
1485 Nagel, Ivan. "Gezähmte Vogelscheuchen." <u>Süddeutsche Zeitung</u>, 9 October 1970, p. 35.

11 / <u>Davor</u> (1970)

1969

1486 Anon. "Hilft ein Striptease dem Stück von Günter Grass auf?" <u>Theater heute</u>, 10, No. 7(1969), 67-68.
1487 Aick, Gerhard. "Günter Grass's New Play: What's Good, What Isn't." <u>Atlas</u>, 18(July 1969), 56-57.
1488 Becker, Hellmut. "Lehrer und Schüler--neu gesehen." <u>Die Zeit</u>, 21 February 1969, p. 24.
1489 Dönhoff, Marion Gräfin. "Der Versuch, ohne Utopie zu leben." <u>Die Zeit</u>, 21 February 1969, p. 24.
1490 Eichholz, Armin. "Soll ein Dackel brennen für Vietnam?" <u>Münchner Merkur</u>, 17 February 1969.
1491 Fröhlich, Hans. "Grass, Opfer seiner Redlichkeit." <u>Stuttgarter Nachrichten</u>, 17 February 1969.
1492 Grack, Günther. "Aus unseren Tagen für unsere Tage." <u>Tagesspiegel</u>, 16 February 1969, p. 5.
1493 Habernoll, Kurt. "Danach die Enttäuschung." <u>Vorwärts</u> (Bonn), 20 February 1969.
1494 Hamm, Peter. "Günter Grass probt die Anpassung." <u>Konkret</u>, No. 5(1969), pp. 50-51.

1495 Hamm, Peter. "Die SPD als Zahnarzt." Neues Forum, 16 (1969), 285.

1496 Hermann, Walter M. "Davor von Grass: Theater-Missverständnis." Hamburger Abendblatt, 17 February 1969.

1497 Hildebrandt, Dieter. "Hamlet zwischen Torte und Tortur." Publik (Frankfurt), 21 February 1969.

1498 Ignée, Wolfgang. "Brennen Dackel nicht? Grass' staatsloyales Saubermann-Drama Davor." Christ und Welt, 21 February 1969, p. 10.

1499 Kaiser, Joachim. "Mini-Hamlet probt Aufstand mit Hund." Süddeutsche Zeitung, 17 February 1969, p. 12.

1500 Karasek, Hellmuth. "Lehrer--von innen und aussen." Theater heute, 10, No. 4(1969), 37.

1501 Karasek, Hellmuth. "Wozu das viele Theater?" Die Zeit (U.S. Edition), 18 February 1969, p. 9.

1502 Karasek, Hellmuth. "Hand aufs Herz bei Günter Grass." Die Zeit, 21 February 1969, p. 24.

1503 Kersten, H.U. "Der Dackel Max wird doch nicht verbrannt." Nürnberger Zeitung, 17 February 1969.

1504 Klotz, Volker. "Zeitstück mit künstlichem Gebiss." Frankfurter Rundschau, 17 February 1969.

1505 Kotschenreuther, Helmut. "Der Dackel Max oder Die Zeit der Anpassung." Kieler Nachrichten, 17 February 1969.

1506 Luft, Friedrich. "Ach, wie krümelt der Schmerz . . ." Die Welt, 17 February 1969.

1507 Michaelis, Rolf. "Auf den Hund gekommen." Frankfurter Allgemeine Zeitung, 17 February 1969.

1508 Moschner, Manfred. "Zwischen den Fronten der Generationen." Kölnische Rundschau, 17 February 1969.

1509 Müller, Liselotte. "Mehr Davor als dahinter." Hannoversche Allgemeine Zeitung, 17 February 1969.

1510 Müller, Wolfgang Johannes. "Bekenntnis eines Greises." Bayern-Kurier (München), 22 February 1969.

1511 Nyssen, Leo. "Nebengeräusche. Günter Grass, Davor." Theater heute, 10, No. 5(1969), 9.

1512 Plavius, Heinz. "Geschwätz verhindert Taten." Neue Deutsche Literatur (Berlin), 17, No. 8(1969), 173-78.

1513 Plunien, Eo. "Grass-Masken im Parkett." Die Welt, 16 April 1969, p. 23.

1514 Plunien, Eo. "Davor mit Nachspiel von Grass." Die Welt, 22 May 1969, p. 21.

1515 Rischbieter, Henning. "Aber wie zwischen sitzen wir drinnen." Theater heute, 10, No. 4(1969), 38-39.

1516 Rumler, Fritz. "Ich werde meinen Hund verbrennen." Der Spiegel, 23(17 February 1969), 145-46.

1517 Schäble, Günter. "Wofür?" Stuttgarter Zeitung, 17 February 1969.

1518 Schüler, Gerhard. "Davor." Göttinger Tageblatt, 17 February 1969.

1519 Schwab-Felisch, Hans. "Vernunft auf der Bühne." Merkur, 23(1969), 306-308.

1520 Sonnemann, Ulrich. "Bitte noch mehr spülen! Zur Topographie von Davor." Theater heute, 10, No. 4(1969), 35-37.

1521 Tank, Kurt Lothar. "Karies-Philosophie und Dackel-Dialektik." Sonntagsblatt, 23 February 1969, p. 23.

1522 Thouet, Peter M. "Der Dackel, die Dicken, die Dummen." Berliner Liberale Zeitung, 7 March 1969.

1523 Unger, Wilhelm. "Günter Grass trainiert für den Wahlkampf." Kölner Stadt-Anzeiger, 17 February 1969.

1524 Wapnewski, Peter. "Danach." Publik, 7 March 1969.

1970

1525 Krumtorad, Paul. "Wieso ist Grass berühmt?" Neues Forum (Wien), 17(1970), 186.

1971

1526 Gussow, Mel. "Novel takes to the stage in Günter Grass' Uptight." New York Times, 24 March 1971.

1527 Kurz, Paul Konrad. "Das verunsicherte Wappentier: Zu Davor und örtlich betäubt von Günter Grass." Stimmen der Zeit, 184(1969), 374-89; rpt. Über moderne Literatur III: Standorte und Deutungen (Frankfurt: Knecht, 1971), pp. 89-112.

1528 Mick. "Uptight." Billboard, 25 March 1971.

1529 Wallmann, Jürgen P. "Davor und was davor war." Die Tat, 24 April 1971, p. 35.

1972

1530 Anon. Booklist, 69(1 November 1972), 225.

1531 Hewes, Henry. "Distal and proximal bite." Saturday Review, 55(20 May 1972), 62-63.

1532 Rischbieter, Henning. "Zu dem Theaterstück Davor von Günter Grass." In: Ich ernenne gewisse Dinge für falsch: Zehn Interpretationen zu Theaterstücken und Hörspielen zeitgenössischer Autoren. Hrsg. Goethe-Institut. Deutsch für Ausländer: Texte zum Unterricht mit Tonbändern. Heft 2. München, 1972, pp. 58-64.

1973

1533 Lange, Victor, and Frances Lange (eds.). "Introduction." Günter Grass, Davor. Student Edition (New York: Harcourt Brace Jovanovich, 1973), pp. 1-13.

V. POETRY

0 / The poetry in general

1955

1534 Stephan, Charlotte. "Junge Autoren unter sich." Der
      Tagesspiegel (Berlin), 17 May 1955.

1960

1535 Wegener, Adolph. "Lyrik und Graphik von Günter Grass."
      Philobiblon, 10(1960), 110-18.

1964

1536 Baier, Lothar. "Gedicht als Schnitt durch die Wirklich-
      keit. Zur Lyrik Günter Grass'." Text + Kritik, No. 1
      (1964), 9-12.

1965

1537 Forster, Leonard. "Heutige deutsche Lyrik von aussen ge-
      sehen." Heidelberger Jahrbücher, 9(1965), 91-101.

1966

1538 Blažek, Bohuslav, and Barbara Špitzová. My 66, 3, No. 3
      (1966), 38-39.

1967

1539 Kurz, Paul K., S.J. "Windhühner ausgefragt: Zur Lyrik
      von Günter Grass." Stimmen der Zeit, 180(1967), 167-81;
      rev. rpt. Über moderne Literatur II: Standorte und Deu-
      tungen (Frankfurt: Knecht, 1969), pp. 237-64.
1540 Short, Susan. "Lyriker." Manchester Guardian, 15 July
      1967, p. 4.

1968

1541 Wieser, Theodor. "Günter Grass." Günter Grass. Porträt
      und Poesie (Neuwied, Berlin: Luchterhand, 1968), pp. 5-51.

1969

1542 Hamburger, Michael. "Introduction." Poems of Günter
      Grass (Harmondsworth: Penguin Books, 1969), pp. 9-13.

1970

1543 Hamburger, Michael. "Moralist and Jester: The Poetry of Günter Grass." Dimension, Special Issue 1970, pp. 75-90; rpt. A. Leslie Willson, A Günter Grass Symposium (1971), pp. 71-86.

1544 Piontek, Heinz. "Günter Grass." Männer die Gedichte machen. Zur Lyrik (Hamburg: Hoffmann & Campe, 1970), pp. 179-202.

1545 Vormweg, Heinrich. "Gedichteschreiber Grass." Akzente, 17(1970), 405-16; rpt. in: Günter Grass, Gesammelte Gedichte (Neuwied: Luchterhand, 1971), pp. 5-18.

1971

1546 Baier, Lothar. "Weder ganz noch gar. Günter Grass und das Laborgedicht." Text + Kritik, No. 1/1a., 4. Aufl. (1971), pp. 67-70.

1546/1 Hinderer, Walter. "Sprache und Methode: Bemerkungen zur politischen Lyrik der sechziger Jahre. Enzensberger, Grass, Fried." Revolte und Experiment: Die Literatur der sechziger Jahre in Ost und West, ed. Wolfgang Paulsen (Heidelberg: Stiehm, 1971), pp. 98-143, esp. 123-32.

1547 Piontek, Heinz. "An-die-Wand-Pinnen. Eine der grossen Irrungen des Günter Grass." Der Literat, 13(1971), 196.

1972

1548 Hatfield, Henry. Books Abroad, 46(1972), 297-98.

1549 Jurgensen, Manfred. "Der Lyriker Günter Grass" (Synopsis). AULLA: Proceedings and papers, 14(1972), 178.

1550 Latzel, Siegbert. "Grass als Lyriker." Interpretationskurse "Moderne Literatur" auf Tonband. Inter-Nationes: Kultureller Tonbanddienst. Beilage. München: Goethe-Institut, 1972, pp. 22-26.

1551 Rühmkorf, Peter. Die Jahre die ihr kennt (Reinbek: Rowohlt, 1972), pp. 106-108.

1552 Wallmann, Jürgen P. "Ausgefragt? Zu den Gesammelten Gedichten von Günter Grass." Die Tat (Zürich), 22 January 1972, p. 31.

1973

1553 Krolow, Karl. "Günter Grass in seinen Gedichten." Grass: Kritik--Thesen--Analysen, ed. Manfred Jurgensen (Bern: Francke, 1973), pp. 11-20.

1974

1554 May, Brigitte Zissel. "Gegenständlichkeit und Weltbild: eine Untersuchung zur Lyrik von Günter Grass." Diss.

Tulane University, 1974. Dissertation Abstracts International, 35(1974), 2283-A.

1975

1555   Raddatz, Fritz J. "Prinzip Zweifel." Frankfurter Allgemeine Zeitung, 1 February 1975.

1 / Die Vorzüge der Windhühner (1956)

1956

1556   Hamm, Peter. "Neue Lyrik." Deutsche Rundschau, 82(1956), 1238-41.
1557   Uhlig, Helmut. "Realitäten, Humor und feine Ironie." Sender Freies Berlin, 2 August 1956; rpt. Gert Loschütz, Von Buch zu Buch (1968), pp. 164-65.

1957

1558   Bobrowski, Johannes. "Die Windhühner." Das Buch von drüben (Berlin), March 1957; rpt. Gert Loschütz, Von Buch zu Buch (1968), p. 165.
1559   Michelsen, Peter. "Moderne Gedichte?" Neue deutsche Hefte, 3(1956/57), 488-90.
1560   Müller, Heiner. "Die Kröte auf dem Gasometer." Neue deutsche Literatur, 5, No. 1(1957), 160-61.

2 / Gleisdreieck (1960)

1960

1561   Nolte, Jost. "Menschen, gequält von dieser Welt." Die Welt (Hamburg), 2 December 1960.

1961

1562   Becker, Jürgen. "Gleisdreieck." Westdeutscher Rundfunk (Köln), 15 February 1961; rpt. Gert Loschütz, Von Buch zu Buch (1968), pp. 166-68.
1563   Krolow, Karl. "Gleisdreieck." Südwestfunk (Baden-Baden), 29 March 1961; rpt. Gert Loschütz, Von Buch zu Buch (1968), pp. 169-71.
1564   Segebrecht, Wulf. "Für prüde Gemüter ungeeignet." Vorwärts (Bonn), 17 February 1961; rpt. Gert Loschütz, Von Buch zu Buch (1968), pp. 168-69.
1565   Singer, Herbert. "Die Nachteile der Windeier." Neue deutsche Hefte, No. 79(1961), pp. 1025-26.

1566 Wieser, Theodor. "Die Hühner des Günter Grass." <u>Du</u>, 21 (May 1961), 54-55.

1962

1567 Salinger, Herman. <u>Books Abroad</u>, 36(Winter 1962), 54.

3 / <u>Selected Poems</u> (1966)

1966

1568 Anon. "Poems of Grass." <u>Times Literary Supplement</u>, 20 January 1966, p. 45.
1569 Anon. "Leaves of Grass." <u>Time</u>, 87(1 April 1966), 103-104.
1570 Anon. <u>Booklist</u>, 62(1 May 1966), 859.
1571 Anon. <u>Choice</u>, 3(September 1966), 524.
1572 Alvarez, A. <u>Observer</u>, 2 January 1966, p. 25.
1573 Carey, John. <u>New Statesman</u>, 71(18 February 1966), 232.
1574 Clements, Robert J. <u>Saturday Review</u>, 49(21 May 1966), 30.
1575 Cox, C.B. "Grass Roots." <u>Spectator</u>, 216(1 April 1966), 411.
1576 Deen, Rosemary F. <u>Commonweal</u>, 84(16 September 1966), 594-95.
1577 Hecht, Anthony. <u>Hudson Review</u>, 19(Summer 1966), 338.
1578 Knight, Max. "Romp through the brambles." <u>New York Times Book Review</u>, 71(14 August 1966), 5.
1579 Martin, Graham. <u>Listener</u>, 75(12 May 1966), 694.
1580 Press, John. <u>Punch</u>, 250(2 February 1966), 175.
1581 Wassermann, Felix M. <u>Library Journal</u>, 91(15 March 1966), 1431.
1582 West, P. <u>Book Week</u>, 8 May 1966, p. 4.

1967

1583 Fraser, G.S. <u>Partisan Review</u>, 34(Winter 1967), 154-55.
1584 Sullivan, Dale H. <u>West Coast Review</u>, 1(Winter 1967), 56-58.

1968

1585 Mueller, Lisel. "German Chronicle." <u>Poetry</u> (Chicago), 111(February 1968), 336-40.

1969

1586 Brownjohn, Alan. <u>New Statesman</u>, 78(15 August 1969), 218.
1587 Furlong, Richard. <u>London Magazine</u>, 9(October 1969), 103-104.

1967

1588 Anon. Times Literary Supplement, 66(28 September 1967), 912.

1589 Clements, R.J. Saturday Review, 50(1 July 1967), 19.

1590 Fried, Erich. "Protestgedichte gegen Protestgedichte." Die Zeit, 18 August 1967.

1591 Fried, Erich. "Ist Ausgefragt fragwürdig?" Konkret (Hamburg), No. 7(1967), pp. 44-45; rpt. Gert Loschütz, Von Buch zu Buch (1968), pp. 183-88.

1592 Fried, Erich. "Hans Mayer, oder der nachhinkende Schweinskopf." Konkret, No. 9(1967), 34-37.

1593 Härtling, Peter. "Gedichte zu Gelegenheiten." Der Spiegel, 21(3 July 1967), 90-91; rpt. Gert Loschütz, Von Buch zu Buch (1968), pp. 181-83; rpt. Literatur im Spiegel, ed. Rolf Becker (Hamburg: Rowohlt, 1969), pp. 224-27.

1594 Hamm, Peter. "Alles Schöne ist schief." Twen (Köln), July 1967.

1595 Heise, Hans-Jürgen. "Zwischen Politik und Literatur." Die Tat (Zürich), 15 July 1967.

1596 Herms, Uwe. "Heute back ich, morgen brau ich, übermorgen . . ." Stuttgarter Zeitung, 8 April 1967.

1597 Jenny, Urs. "Im Vakuum heiter bleiben." Die Weltwoche (Zürich), 19 May 1967, p. 26.

1598 Jürgens, Martin. "Günter Grass: Ausgefragt." Neue Rundschau, 78(1967), 484-90.

1599 Kaiser, Joachim. "Der gelassene Grass." Süddeutsche Zeitung (München), 27 April 1967; rpt. Gert Loschütz, Von Buch zu Buch (1968), pp. 174-76.

1600 Kielinger, Thomas. "Günter Grass: Ausgefragt." Neue deutsche Hefte, 14, No. 4(1967), 140-43.

1601 Kraft, Peter. "Vergleiche und ähnliche Alleskleber." Oberösterreichische Nachrichten (Linz), 22 June 1967.

1602 Krauschner, Helga. "Wohin mit der Wut?" Die Furche (Wien), 8 April 1967.

1603 Krolow, Karl. "Alles Schöne ist schief." Hannoversche Allgemeine, 15 April 1967.

1604 Lentz, Michael. "Gedichte in Moll." Westdeutsche Allgemeine (Essen), 3 June 1967.

1605 Maier, Wolfgang. "Die Unruhe um der Ruhe willen." Berliner Morgenpost, 21 July 1967.

1606 Mayer, Hans. "Das lyrische Tagebuch des Günter Grass." Der Tagesspiegel (Berlin), 23 July 1967, p. 35.

1607 Nolte, Jost. "Baltisch, tückisch, stubenwarm." Die Welt, 13 April 1967.

1608 Piontek, Heinz. "Ein Gedicht und sein Autor." Süddeutsche Zeitung (München), 7 December 1967.

1609 Reich-Ranicki, Marcel. "Neue Gedichte von Günter Grass." Die Zeit, 19 May 1967, p. 24.

1610 Reich-Ranicki, Marcel. "Günter Grass: Ausgefragt." Literatur der kleinen Schritte (München: Piper, 1967), pp. 272-78.

1611 Schultz, Uwe. "Auskunft über die Ohnmacht." Frankfurter Rundschau, 12 August 1967, p. vi.

1612 Segebrecht, Dietrich. "Dialektik oder das Vorbild der Kochkunst." Frankfurter Allgemeine Zeitung, 14 March 1967.

1613 Vormweg, Heinrich. "Keine Antwort für Günter Grass." Civis, 13, No. 1(1967), 29-30.

1614 Weyrauch, Wolfgang. "Ausgefragt: Was heisst das?" Tribüne (Frankfurt), 6(1967), 2482-83.

1615 Zacher, Ewald. "Gedichte, aber nicht als Alibi." Wort und Wahrheit, 22(1967), 630-31.

1968

1616 Schneider, Peter. "Individuelle Sachlichkeit." Kürbiskern (München), No. 1(1968), pp. 169-72.

1617 Wolf, Gerhard. "Neue Bücher: Besprechungen." Neue deutsche Literatur, 16, No. 9(1968), 166.

1969

1618 Kraft, Werner. "Kleine Gedichte von Günter Grass." Merkur, 23(1969), 492-94.

1971

1619 Arnold, Heinz Ludwig. "'Zorn Ärger Wut.' Anmerkungen zu den politischen Gedichten in Ausgefragt." Text + Kritik, No. 1/1a, 4. Aufl. (1971), pp. 71-73; rpt. Grass: Kritik--Thesen--Analysen, ed. Manfred Jurgensen (Bern: Francke, 1973), pp. 103-106.

5 / New Poems (1968)

1968

1620 Anon. Publishers Weekly, 193(26 February 1968), 166.

1621 Anon. Kirkus Service, 36(15 March 1968), 369.

1622 Anon. Booklist, 65(1 September 1968), 32.

1623 Wassermann, Felix M. Library Journal, 93(15 April 1968), 1638.

1969

1624 Szanto, George H. "Tired muse." Catholic World, 208 (March 1969), 274-75.

1973

1625 Beckmann, Heinz. "Masurisches Handchenvoll." <u>Rheinischer</u>
Merkur, 7 December 1973, p. 40.
1626 Fabian, Rainer. "Von Schweinsköpfen und Augäpfeln." <u>Die</u>
Welt, 11 October 1973, p. XIII.
1627 Zimmer, Dieter E. "Grass' Marienchronik." <u>Die Zeit</u>, 12
October 1973, p. 9.

1974

1628 Anon. "Kaum der Rede wert." <u>Die Presse</u>, 30/31 March
1974, p. 21.
1629 Anon. Publishers Weekly, 206(22 July 1974), 67.
1630 Anon. <u>Kirkus Reviews</u>, 42(15 August 1974), 935.
1631 Anon. <u>Library Journal</u>, 99(August 1974), 1933.
1632 Anon. <u>Book World</u>, 1 September 1974, p. 3.
1633 Anon. <u>Booklist</u>, 71(1 October 1974), 131.
1634 Anon. <u>New Republic</u>, 171(23 November 1974), 43.

1975

1635 Anon. <u>Choice</u>, 11(February 1975), 1762.
1636 Anon. <u>Virginia</u> Quarterly Review, 51(Spring 1975), lvii.

7 / Individual poems

1961

1637 Völker, Klaus. "'Kinderlied' von Günter Grass." <u>Sender</u>
Freies Berlin, 15 October 1961; rpt. Gert Loschütz, <u>Von</u>
<u>Buch zu Buch</u> (1968), pp. 172-73.

1963

1638 Seidler, Ingo. "Rainer Maria Rilke und Günter Grass:
zwei Gedichte oder eines?" <u>International Arthur Schnitz-</u>
ler Research Association Journal (Lexington, Ky.), 2, No.
4(1963), 4-10 ("Kinderlied").

1965

1639 Metzger-Hirt, Erika. "Günter Grass, 'Askese': Eine Interpretation." <u>Monatshefte</u>, 57(1965), 283-90.
1640 Riha, Karl. <u>Moritat, Song</u>, Bänkelsang: Zur Geschichte der
moderne Ballade (Göttingen: Sachse und Pohl, 1965), pp.
159-66 ("Annabel Lee").
1641 Weber, Werner. "Günter Grass: 'Brandmauern'." <u>Tagebuch</u>

eines Lesers. Bemerkungen und Aufsätze zur Literatur (Olten, Freiburg i. Br.: Walter, 1965), pp. 88-92.

1966

1642 Forster, Leonard and Günter Grass. "Kirschen." Doppelinterpretationen. Das zeitgenössische deutsche Gedicht zwischen Autor und Leser, ed. Hilde Domin (Frankfurt, Bonn: Athenäum, 1966), pp. 276-80.

1968

1643 Bräutigam, K. "Günter Grass: 'Freitag'." Moderne deutsche Balladen. ("Erzählgedichte"). Versuche zu ihrer Deutung (Frankfurt: Diesterweg, 1968), pp. 94-99.

1970

1644 Kienecker, Friedrich. "Günter Grass: 'Im Ei'." Der Mensch in der modernen Lyrik: Eine Handreichung zur Interpretation (Essen: Ludgerus Verlag, 1970), pp. 97-105.
1645 Kopplin, Wolfgang. "Zu einem Gedicht von Günter Grass." Welt und Wort, 25(1970), 43-44 ("Schulpause").

VI. THEORETICAL, POLITICAL, AND MISCELLANEOUS WRITINGS

1 / Über das Selbstverständliche (1968)

1966

1646 Hamburger, Michael. Encounter, 26(April 1966), 62-64.

1967

1647 Kaiser, Carl Christian. "Günter Grass gibt zu denken." Stuttgarter Zeitung, 31 May 1967.

1968

1648 Anon. "For Freedom." Times Literary Supplement, 67(11 April 1968), 367.
1649 Boveri, Margret. "Variationen des Selbstverständlichen." Merkur (Stuttgart), 22(1968), 765-71.
1650 Engert, Jürgen. "Dennoch? Dennoch? Günter Grass, Über das Selbstverständliche." Der Monat, 20, No. 238(1968), 72-74.
1651 Hornung, Werner. "Günter Grass, Über das Selbstverständliche." Tribüne, 7(1968), 2843-44.

1652 Kielinger, Thomas. Review of Über das Selbstverständ-
      liche. Neue deutsche Hefte, 15, No. 3(1968), pp. 216-18.
1653 Kniffler, Carsten. "Die 'Rede von der Gewöhnung' von
      Günter Grass im Deutschunterricht." Gesellschaft, Staat,
      Erziehung (Frankfurt/Main), 13, No. 6(1968), 365-70.
1654 Krüger, Horst. "Schwierigkeiten beim Parteiergreifen. Die
      politischen Texte von Günter Grass." Die Zeit, 23, No. 22
      (1968), 23-24.
1655 Müller, Manfred. "Prinzip Vernunft--enttäuschte Hoff-
      nung." Frankfurter Rundschau, 29 June 1968, p. V.
1656 Schroers, Rolf. "Grass in der Stunde der Gefahr." Christ
      und Welt, 5 April 1968, 39.
1657 Wallmann, Jürgen P. "Ein Musterschüler des Reformismus:
      Zu den politischen Schriften von Günter Grass." Die Tat,
      21 September 1968, p. 34.

      1969

1658 Arnold, Heinz Ludwig. "Grosses Ja und Kleines Nein:
      Fragen zur politischen Wirkung des Günter Grass." Frank-
      furter Rundschau, 8 March 1969, (Feuilleton:) p. IV; rpt.
      Brauchen wir noch die Literatur? (Düsseldorf: Bertelsmann,
      1972), pp. 81-86; rpt. Grass: Kritik--Thesen--Analysen,
      ed. Manfred Jurgensen (Bern: Francke, 1973), p. 87-96.
1659 Kauf, Robert. "Politik und Aufklärung." German Quarter-
      ly, 42(1969), 765-66.
1660 Wallmann, Jürgen P. "Günter Grass, Über das Selbstver-
      ständliche." Zeitwende, 40(1969), 130-32.
1661 Wintzen, René. "Les intellectuels allemands et la poli-
      tique. L'écrivain est-il un bouffon?" Le Monde, 28 June
      1969.

      2 / Über meinen Lehrer Döblin (1968)

      1966

1662 Sommer, D. "Im Kampf mit der schwarzen Köchin: Zu einer
      Rede Günter Grassens." Ich schreibe (Leipzig), No. 1
      (1966).

      1967

1663 E., H. "Alfred Döblin geehrt." Aufbau (New York), 28
      July 1967.
1664 Roemer, Friedrich. "Kritisch anverwandelt, liebevoll
      distanziert. Günter Grass sprach zu Alfred Döblins 10.
      Todestag in der Akademie der Künste." Die Welt, 10 July
      1967.
1665 Stow. "Günter Grass und 'sein Lehrer.' Ein Plädoyer für
      Döblin." Badische Zeitung (Freiburg i. Br.), 25 July 1967.

1666 Wirsing, Sybille. "Alfred Döblin, der Unbekannte. Günter Grass sprach in der Akademie der Künste." Der Tagesspiegel (Berlin), 9 July 1967.

1968

1667 Holthusen, Hans Egon. "Narren als Dauermieter: Günter Grass, Über meinen Lehrer Döblin und andere Vorträge." Christ und Welt, 6 December 1968, p. 47.

1970

1668 Henisch, Peter. "Günter Grass: Über meinen Lehrer Döblin und andere Vorträge." Literatur und Kritik, 1970, pp. 246-48.

1973

1669 Jurgensen, Manfred. "Die gegenständliche Muse: 'Der Inhalt als Widerstand'." Grass: Kritik—Thesen—Analysen (Bern: Francke, 1973), pp. 199-210.

3 / Speak Out! (1969)

1670 Ascherson, Neal. "Raw nerves." New York Review of Books, 13(20 November 1969), 16-21.
1671 Harrington, Michael. "The politics of Günter Grass." Atlantic, 223(April 1969), 129-31.
1672 Maddocks, Melvin. "You don't have to be dull to be a moderate." Christian Science Monitor, 29 May 1969, p. 15.
1673 Mander, John. "Germany's voice of democracy." The Guardian, 20 September 1969.
1674 Prittie, Terence. "Speak Out!" New York Times Book Review, 25 May 1969, p. 6.
1675 Simon, John. "A call for radical democracy." Book World, 3(18 May 1969), 3.
1676 Sokolow, Raymond A. "The voice of Grass." Newsweek, 73 (26 May 1969), 120, 125.
1677 Toynbee, Philip. "A torch for Brandt." The Observer Review, 7 September 1969.

4 / Der Bürger und seine Stimme (1974)

1974

1678 Krüger, Horst. "Der Bürger Günter Grass und seine kritische Stimme." Frankfurter Allgemeine Zeitung, 17 October 1974, p. 26.
1679 Luft, Friedrich. "Ein Prophet erkennt sich." Die Welt,

10 October 1974, p. 11.

1680 Schmid, Waldemar. "Leserliches Stenogramm einer Stim-
      mungslage." Badische Zeitung, 28/29 December 1974.

1975

1681 Kurz, Paul Konrad. "Bürgers Blechtrommler." Deutsche
      Zeitung, 7 February 1975, p. 12.
1682 Steffen, Jochen. "Gleiche Brüder auf verschiedenen Wegen:
      Günter Grass und Hans Magnus Enzensberger als politische
      Redner, Kommentatoren und Essayisten." Die Zeit, 31
      January 1975, p. 15.

Entries numbered lower than 500 refer to PRIMARY material. Entries numbered 500 and higher refer to SECONDARY material.

Göpfert, Peter Hans, 412, 414, 415
Görtz, Franz Josef, 505, 506, 514-15, 656
Gössmann, Wilhelm, 403, 1240
Goetze, Albrecht, 1155, 1158
Gombrowicz, Witold, 557
Gonzalez, Carmen, 254
Goradza, Joseph, 281
Grack, Günther, 1348, 1492
Grathoff, Dirk, 513, 1459
Grau, Werner, 525
Graves, Peter J., 920
Gray, P.E., 1216
Gregory, Horace, 829
Gregory, Sister M., 1478
Greiff, Trygve, 224, 241
Grimm, Reinhold, 1455
Grimmelshausen, J.J.C. von, 891
Grözinger, Wolfgang, 790, 973, 1088
Grumbach, Doris, 830
Grunenberg, Nina, 621
Grunfeld, Fred, 831
Günzel, Manfred, 526
Gugisch, Peter, 521
Gussow, Mel, 1526
Gutwillig, Robert, 992
Haberl, Franz P., 1217
Habernoll, Kurt, 1387, 1493
Hacks, Peter, 596
Härtling, Peter, 1048, 1593
Häsler, 371
Häussermann, Bernhard, 1049
Hahnl, Hans Heinz, 1050, 1388, 1389
Hamburger, Michael, 44, 47, 296, 298, 299, 302, 305, 308, 309, 312, 708, 1542, 1543, 1646
Hamm, Peter, 608, 765, 1390, 1494, 1495, 1556, 1594
Handke, Peter, 129
Hanson, William P., 832
Haro, Ramón de, 323
Harrington, Michael, 1671
Hartl, Edwin, 1238, 1252
Hartlaub, Geno, 347, 766
Hartmann, Rainer, 1391, 1392
Hartung, Günter, 731

Hartung, Karl, 136
Hartung, Rudolf, 791, 944, 1051
Hasenclever, Walter, 333
Hassner, Pierre, 622
Hatfield, Henry, 714, 724, 1548
Hayman, Ronald, 390, 690, 1456
Hecht, Anthony, 1577
Hecht, Werner, 1393
Heinemann, Frank, 407
Heise, Hans-Jürgen, 1595
Heiseler, Bernt von, 704
Heissenbüttel, Helmut, 522
Heller, Joseph, 717
Henisch, Peter, 1668
Henn, Walter, 70
Hensel, Georg, 945
Herburger, Günter, 664
Herchenröder, Jan, 792, 1052
Hermann, Walter M., 1447, 1496
Herms, Uwe, 1596
Hewes, Henry, 1448, 1531
Hildebrandt, Dieter, 1394, 1497
Hill, William B., 1110
Himmel, Hellmuth, 993
Hinde, Thomas, 994
Hinderer, Walter, 1546/1
Hingst, Wolfgang, 1282
Hobson, Harold, 646
Hochmann, Sandra, 833
Höck, Wilhelm, 1177
Höfer, Werner, 357
Höller, Franz, 946
Höllerer, Walter, 86, 709, 767, 793
Hoffmann, Gerhard H., 623
Hoffmann, Jens, 341, 558, 1395
Hohoff, Curt, 1053, 1089, 1253
Holmberg, Nils, 229
Holme, Christopher, 284
Holthusen, Hans Egon, 577, 597, 853, 1254, 1667
Honsza, Norbert, 598, 647, 868
Hope, Francis, 1218

Klunker, H., 380
Klunker, Heinz, 951, 1091
Kniffler, Carsten, 1653
Knight, Max, 1578
Knudsen, Jørgen, 611
Kohout, Pavel, 101, 139,
    219, 313
Kôji, Nakano, 267
Konrad, H., 1405
Kopplin, Wolfgang, 1645
Korn, Karl, 952
Kotschenreuther, Hellmuth,
    349, 1406, 1484, 1505
Kozarynowa, Zofia, 837
Krättli, Anton, 1187
Kraft, Martin, 1309
Kraft, Peter, 1601
Kraft, Werner, 1618
Kraus, Wolfgang, 772
Krauschner, Helga, 1602
Krauss, Erika, 370
Kremer, Manfred, 923
Kreuder, Ernst, 713
Kriegel, Leonard, 1221
Krolow, Karl, 773, 1553,
    1563, 1603
Krüger, Horst, 544, 626,
    627, 628, 650, 668, 1188,
    1256, 1654, 1678
Kruntorad, Paul, 1525
Kuczynski, Jürgen, 1451
Kuhn, Heinrich, 860
Kunkel, Francis L., 1005
Kurth, Liselotte E., 1159
Kurz, Paul Konrad, 629, 630,
    1092, 1189, 1190, 1283,
    1527, 1539, 1681
Kusenberg, Kurt, 887
Labhardt, Robert, 669
Lange, Frances, 26, 1533
Lange, Victor, 26, 1533
Langfelder, Paul, 1093
Lattmann, Dieter, 392, 562
Latzel, Siegbert, 1550
Lebeau, Jean, 677
Lebeer, Irmelin, 381
Leber, Hugo, 797
Lehmann, Lutz, 1010
Leiser, Erwin, 345, 1407
Lentz, Michael, 1604
Lenz, Siegfried, 113

Leonard, Irène, 631, 678,
    684, 692
Leonhardt, Rudolf, 545, 632
Lerchbacher, Hans, 410
Lerner, Laurence, 815
Leroy, Robert, 892, 924
Lettau, Reinhard, 599
Levay, Z. John, 1142
Levine, Paul, 995
Levitt, Morton Paul, 861
Lewald, H.E., 807
Lewis, Norman Howard, 750
Liljegren, Eva, 270
Linder, Gisela, 1310
Lindley, Denver, 838
Lindroth, James R., 1116,
    1222
Linke, Rainer, 382
Lipinsky-Gottersdorf, Hans,
    904
Lodge, David, 816
Lörinc, Peter, 856
Loetscher, Hugo, 326, 794
Lohner, Edgar, 2, 1022
Lord, Elizabeth G., 306
Lorenzen, Rudolf, 368
Lortholary, Bernard, 315,
    319
Loschütz, Gert, 501, 512
Loy, Leo, 391
Lucke, Hans, 1023
Luft, Friedrich, 1338,
    1349, 1350, 1354, 1408,
    1506, 1679
Luuk, Ernst, 394
Luyken, Sonja, 1328
Macauley, Robie, 275
McDonnel, T.P., 1117
McGovern, Hugh, 839, 996
McGuinness, Frank, 1143
Maddocks, Melvin, 1118,
    1284, 1672
Maier, Hansgeorg, 798
Maier, Wolfgang, 975, 1605
Maloff, Saul, 1119
Mandel, Siegfried, 720
Mander, John, 1479, 1673
Manger, Hermien, 244
Manheim, Ralph, 226, 245,
    260, 269, 274, 277, 280,
    283, 285, 290, 295, 318

Ryszka, Franciszek, 1124
s.s., 1311
Salinger, Herman, 1567
Salyámosy, Miklós, 586
Saña Alcón, Heleno, 293
Sann, Gisela, 756
Sárközy, Elga, 252
Schäble, Günter, 363, 1517
Schallück, Paul, 166
Schauder, Karlheinz, 977, 1289
Scherman, David E., 564
Schiller, Karl, 212
Schimansky, Gerd, 1194
Schimming, W., 1421
Schlocker, Georges, 1422
Schlossarek, G. Dieter, 958
Schmid, Christof, 404
Schmid, Waldemar, 1680
Schmidt, Arno, 116
Schmidt, Aurel, 1261
Schmidt, Josef H.K., 565
Schmidt, Rudolf, 521
Schmolze, Gerhard, 1290
Schneider, Peter, 1616
Schnurre, Wolfdietrich, 110
Schöffler, Heinz, 48
Schönfelder, Fritz, 566
Scholz, Günther, 1262
Scholz, Hans, 1069, 1195, 1263
Schonauer, Franz, 776
Schott, Webster, 1423
Schreiber, Mathias, 695
Schrieber, Ludwig Gabriel, 223, 935
Schroers, Rolf, 1656
Schüler, Alfred, 1424
Schüler, Gerhard, 959, 1330, 1518
Schütte, Ernst, 568, 569
Schütz, Klaus, 141
Schultz, Uwe, 1611
Schumann, Willy, 871
Schuur, Koos, 232, 259
Schuur-Kaspers, C., 268
Schwab-Felisch, Hans, 1196, 1264, 1340, 1425, 1442, 1519
Schwarz, Wilhelm Johannes, 409, 502, 635, 687

Schweckendiek, Adolf, 1026
Schwedhelm, Karl, 960, 1070
Scott, Nathan A., Jr., 636
Secci, Lia, 234
Segebrecht, Dietrich, 978, 1072, 1197, 1612
Segebrecht, Wulf, 1564
Seghers, Anna, 109
Seidler, Ingo, 1638
Seifert, Walter, 908
Seiler, Bernd W., 1464
Sekal, Zbyněk, 251
Serke, Jürgen, 330
Shakespeare, William, 117, 321, 895, 1375, 1437
Sharfman, William L., 872
Shaw, George Bernard, 1460
Short, Susan, 1540
Shorter, Kingsley, 1226
Shuttleworth, Martin, 1125
Siegler, Wilhelm, 1035
Siering, Joachim, 1071
Silver, Lee, 1474
Simmerding, Gertrud, 404
Sinyavsky, Andrei D., 221, 695
Simon, John, 848, 1126, 1675
Singer, Herbert, 1565
Šliažas, Rimvydas, 680, 1162
Smith, M.A., 882
Smith, William James, 1362
Sodeikat, Ernst, 726
Sokolow, Raymond A., 1676
Solotaroff, Theodore, 1127
Solzhenitsyn, Aleksandr I., 221
Sommer, D., 1662
Sonnemann, Ulrich, 1520
Sosnoski, M.K., 909
Spaethling, Robert H., 1027
Sparks, Kimberly, 316
Spelman, Franz, 537
Spender, Stephen, 817, 1000, 1001, 1128
Špitzová, Barbara, 1538
Springer, Axel C., 100, 592
Spycher, Peter, 1355
Stach, Jiří, 286
Stammen, Theo, 1072
Stauch-von Quitzow, Wolf-gang, 1369

DATE DUE

FEB 26 1999			